Oh, Baby!

Precious, Adorable, Lovable Ideas
for Scrapbooking Baby Pages

FROM THE EDITORS OF MEMORY MAKERS BOOKS

Memory Makers Books
Cincinnati, Ohio

www.mycraftivity.com

12 11 10 09 08   5 4 3 2 1

Distributed in Canada by Fraser Direct
100 Armstrong Avenue
Georgetown, ON, Canada L7G 5S4
Tel: (905) 877-4411

Distributed in the U.K. and Europe by David & Charles
Brunel House, Newton Abbot, Devon, TQ12 4PU, England
Tel: (+44) 1626 323200, Fax: (+44) 1626 323319
E-mail: postmaster@davidandcharles.co.uk

Distributed in Australia by Capricorn Link
P.O. Box 704, S. Windsor, NSW 2756 Australia
Tel: (02) 4577-3555

Library of Congress Cataloging-in-Publication Data
Oh, baby! : precious, adorable, lovable ideas for scrapbooking baby pages / editors of Memory Makers Books. – 1st ed.
    p. cm.
  Includes index.
  ISBN 978-1-59963-021-2 (alk. paper)
  1. Photograph albums. 2. Scrapbooks. 3. Baby books. I. Memory Makers Books.
TR501.O34 2008
745.593–dc22

                    2007045989

F+W PUBLICATIONS, INC.
www.fwpublications.com

Photo Credits
All photos ©iStockphoto.com/[artist]
p. 114 (photos): Lauri Wiberg
p. 115 (cutting tools): Robert Dant
p. 115 (adhesive): Johanna Goodyear
p. 115 (adhesive roller): Mark Bolton
p. 116 (spiral album): Sami Ridwan

EDITOR *Kristin Boys*

DESIGNER *Kelly O'Dell*

ART COORDINATOR *Eileen Aber*

PRODUCTION COORDINATOR *Matt Wagner*

PHOTOGRAPHERS *Adam Henry, Adam Leigh-Manuell and John Carrico, Alias Imaging LLC; Tim Grondin, Christine Polomsky, Melanie Warner*

STYLIST *Nora Martini*

WRITER *Heather Eades*

Contributing Artists

Yvette Adams
Ruth Akers
Jennifer Armentrout
Monica BaconRind
Heather Bowser
Shannon Brouwer
Katie Burnett
Mindy Bush
Claude Campeau
Shirley Chai
Staci Compher
Ann Costen
Terri Davenport
Kathie Davis
Corinne Delis
Lori DiAnni
Sheila Doherty
Melanie Douthit
Jen Erickson
Leah Farquharson
Andrea Friebus
Vicky Gibson

Michelle Gowland
Maegan Hall
Greta Hammond
Kara Henry
Lisa Hoel
Melissa Kelley
Amy Knepper
Sue Kristoff
Marci Lambert
Robyn Lantz
Paola López-Araiza Osante
Deborah Mahnken
April Massad
Jennifer Mayer
Trina McClune
Athena Mejia
Stacey Michaud
Cyndi Michener
Sandi Minchuk
Kelly Noel
Kelly O'Dell
Sheila Penner

Christine Pfeiffer
Mandie Pierce
Annette Pixley
Lana Rappette
Jennifer Richards
Mou Saha
Tania Cordova Shaw
Linda Sobolewski
Maureen Spell
Debbie Standard
Colleen Stearns
Shannon Taylor
Cindy Tobey
Lisa Tutman-Oglesby
Samantha Walker
Courtney Walsh
Jaime Warren
Andrea Wiebe
Amy Williams
Sherry Wright
Deena Wuest

introduction

Oh, baby! Who can resist that bald head, those chubby legs and adorably pink cheeks? You get a whiff of that intoxicating scent—boom! Gotta have that "baby fix." Whether baby love is for your own child, a grandchild or a friend's little one, you stand in awe at that onesie-clad illustration of all things innocent, pure and oh, so sweet.

But that sweet little one won't stay little for long. Babies all too quickly grow up. Precious moments are fleeting and emotions are overwhelming. Scrapbook layouts treasuring this time are the perfect and precious way to make babyhood last and to share the love that fills your heart to its brim. Impatient anticipation, milestones through baby's first year, the tricks and quirks, all those things that make your baby uniquely yours—they will all find a home on adorable pages guaranteed to make you smile for years to come.

Be inspired by the pages in this book that cherish all kinds of moments and capture loads of memories. Whether you are looking for fresh layout ideas or are scrapping for the first time, let *Oh, Baby!* be your guide to creating lovable layouts that capture the center of your heart.

chapter

ONE

anticipation

From the moment that hint of a second line appears on your pregnancy test, your life is forever changed and blessed. And then you wait. And wait and wait and wait. Waiting for your miracle to arrive is a surreal experience until those first flutters appear. But then you wonder, was it the little one doing acrobatics inside, or was it simply butterflies of joyful anticipation? As your belly grows with each passing month, so too does your list of questions, worries, hopes and dreams. With thoughts flying at you nearly as quick as the heartbeat on the sonogram screen, you need to create memory pages to provide a resting place for your mind, and to help organize the mass of emotions that expands right along with your waistband. And as you and your little one pore over these layouts of great expectation in the years to come, you are able to show your child just how much your baby was loved even before being born.

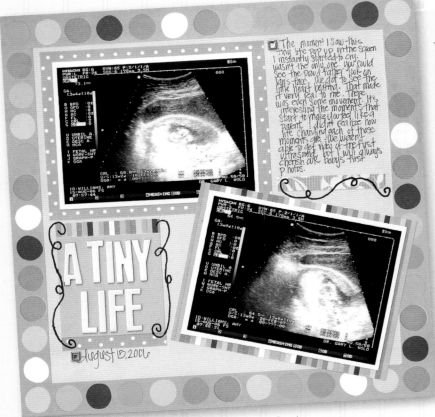

Your baby's first photos may not look like much to the untrained eye, but to proud parents to be, these images showcase the movements of a miracle. Amy's playful and energetic patterns in pastel colors keep this layout's look baby soft while celebrating the motion of a new life's tiny heartbeat. As a family grows, that often means cutting costs. Try Amy's technique to extend the life of patterned paper: Trim a border from the paper, and save the rest of the page for another layout.

A TINY LIFE *by Amy Williams*

Supplies: Cardstock; patterned paper (Chatterbox, KI Memories, Scenic Route); chipboard letters (Heidi Swapp); rhinestone brads (Making Memories); Misc: pen

Those amazing ultrasound images are way too precious to be tucked away inside some box, but can keep people guessing when it comes to creating pages. By setting a couple of first glimpses of your baby on a page against negative space, you allow the power of new life to make a dramatic impact. Courtney expressed her joy for her little miracle's first photo shoot with just a handful of coordinating die-cuts, patterned paper and buttons.

CAN'T WAIT TO MEET YOU
by Courtney Walsh

Supplies: Cardstock; die-cut accents, patterned paper (Fancy Pants); letter stickers (Arctic Frog); buttons (Autumn Leaves); Misc: adhesive foam, floss, pen

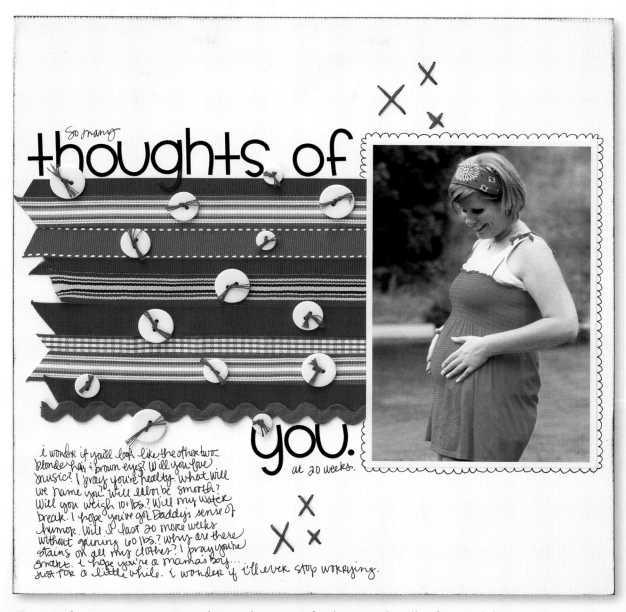

so many
thoughts of
you.
at 20 weeks.

i wonder if you'll look like the other two... blonde hair & brown eyes? will you love music? i pray you're healty. what will we name you? will labor be smooth? will you weigh 10+lbs? will my water break. i hope you've got Daddy's sense of humor. will i last 20 more weeks without gaining 60 lbs.? why are there stains on all my clothes? i pray you're smart. i hope you're a mama's boy... just for a little while. i wonder if i'll ever stop worrying.

Forty weeks can seem an eternity when you're waiting for that sweet bundle of joy; and the questions, the hopes and the wonders never cease! A layout is the perfect place to release those heartfelt emotions in a simple, handwritten, free-flowing journaling block, while keeping the focus of the page on your image. Enhance the casual look of your photo with a staggered assortment of coordinating ribbons embellished by hand stitching and buttons.

THOUGHTS OF YOU *by Courtney Walsh*

Supplies: Cardstock; letter stickers (Doodlebug); ribbon (Offray, Wrights); Misc: buttons, floss, ink, pen

Natural beauty is what pregnancy is all about, showcasing femininity at its finest. Design a page, such as Jaime's, utilizing earth tones and bohemian prints to rejoice in arriving at the final stretch (mark!) of this miraculous journey. A large floral element, enhanced with shimmers and shine is all the glamour a page like this needs to capture the aesthetics of a mama-to-be. Space set between journaling strips keeps a page clean and uncluttered, while torn edges around a photo block soften the look.

8 MONTHS *by Jaime Warren*

Supplies: Patterned paper (My Mind's Eye); chipboard letters, small rhinestones (Heidi Swapp); transparency overlay (Hambly); sticker accents (7gypsies)

Capture the soft, sweet feelings and multi-layered emotions of expectancy on a layout like Trina's, utilizing vibrant colors, energetic die-cut shapes and playful buttons. By clustering your page embellishments on one side of the design, you can balance out a large focal point photo. Pull the look together with a bracket that serves as a unifying element and emphasizes a pregnant belly.

37 WEEKS *by Trina McClune*

Supplies: Cardstock; glitter bracket, chipboard letters and tiles, flower, patterned paper (Junkitz); buttons (Autumn Leaves, KI Memories, Junkitz); Misc: acrylic paint, felt, floss, pen

The barrage of questions a mother-to-be has swimming through her mind can be overwhelming at times. Give those thoughts, concerns, worries and wonders a place to rest on an energetic design such as Ruth's. By layering torn patterned paper circles with circular stamps in a coordinating print, you can capture the nonstop movement of never-ending brain activity. Print simple journaling strips in coordinating colors to contrast with the busyness of a page.

I WONDER? *by Ruth Akers*

Supplies: Cardstock; patterned paper, stamps (Paper Salon); brads, letter stickers (American Crafts); Misc: acrylic paint, adhesive foam, thread

positively
glowing

Here is my little sister Veronica, at 8 months pregnant and all I can see in this photo I took of her is how she is positively glowing.

2/07

We all would like to bottle that amazing glow that most mothers-to-be exude. However, until someone develops a formula for such a look of health and beauty, capture this phenomenon on pages that beam with the joy of motherhood. A single black-and-white photo shines when set against glowing colors. Vibrant paper and a few flower embellishments enhanced by coordinating brads are all that is needed to play up the positive energy of the photo.

GLOWING
by Linda Sobolewski

Supplies: Cardstock; patterned paper (A2Z); felt flower and letters, rub-on letters (American Crafts); Misc: brads, pen, silk flowers

*Sh*ow that glow!

Whether your glow is hot or not, you can still get a great pregnancy photo. Try these techniques:

- *Go Black and White*—Use black-and-white film, or simply convert photos using photo editing software.

- *Take the Photos Yourself*—If you feel timid about exposing your naked belly in front of others, set up your own photo shoot, relying on your trusty tripod and timed shutter release.

- *Embrace Your Curves*—Try shooting images of your belly from various angles. By turning your baby's home to a three-quarters view, you'll get beautiful images enhanced by this angle.

- *Relax!*—Play calming music, light scented candles and relax your hands on your belly.

- *Make It a Family Affair*—Get the whole family in on the act. Overlap your husband's hands with yours, or shoot images of siblings-in-waiting gathered around.

the so-called pregnancy glow?

It's up for debate.

headaches

dry skin

heartburn

backache

swollen hands

gut-wrenching kicks

hip & nerve pain

ligament pain

separating pelvic bones

leg cramps

edema

36 weeks

Add to that 40 extra pounds, running to the bathroom every 20 minutes and waddling like a duck. To say I feel less than "glowing" would be an understatement! Not even born yet and you're already a troublemaker! I wouldn't go through this kind of torture for just anyone, ya know. But for you, sweetie, I'd do it a hundred times over.

While many expecting mothers quickly give away their secret with that infamous glow, others find themselves waiting the entire nine months to radiate something other than acne, backaches and varicose veins. Deena created a light-hearted layout to play-up the unpleasant effects of pregnancy. Image editing software allows you to overlay directive lines on your focal point photo, as Deena did here, to highlight the areas of each pregnancy annoyance, while stacked photo frames provide visual interest. Using a curvaceous brushstroke softens an otherwise graphic design.

GLOW? *by Deena Wuest*

Supplies: Image editing software (Adobe); page kit by Leora Sanford (Designer Digitals); frames by Katie Pertiet (Designer Digitals); brush set by Anna Aspnes (Designer Digitals); Misc: Avant Garde and Impact fonts

Unless labor is scheduled, you never know when your little addition will decide to arrive. So always keep a camera handy those last few weeks before delivery to capture the emotion of anticipation. Soft, subtle colors and minimal embellishments allow the raw beauty of the moment you've waited nine (plus!) months for to radiate from your last images. Use round and feminine flourishes, as Amy does here, to balance out and highlight the beauty of a baby belly in its final hours.

SO GLAMOROUS *by Amy Williams*

Supplies: Cardstock; patterned paper (Chatterbox); chipboard letters, journaling accents, photo corners (Heidi Swapp); rhinestones, stamp (Making Memories); Misc: acrylic paint, pen

Capturing the experience of pregnancy in a single layout may seem like a daunting task. However, as Samantha demonstrates, one large, curvaceous element packs a powerful, yet tender punch when set against the contrasting lines of a journaling block. Choose a font that will emphasize the subject of your page, and with a little computer software play, you can easily create a bold title that can serve as a dynamic balance to any page design.

MOTHER AND CHILD
by Samantha Walker

Supplies: Image editing software (Adobe); Misc: Garamond and University fonts, scanned paper flowers

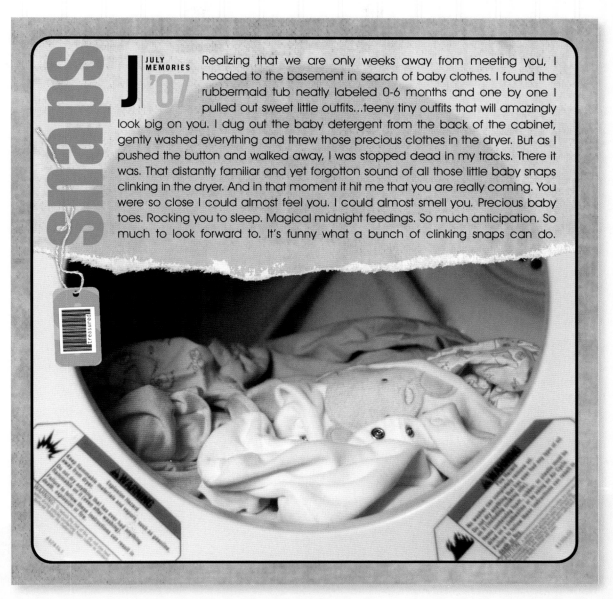

snaps

J JULY MEMORIES '07

Realizing that we are only weeks away from meeting you, I headed to the basement in search of baby clothes. I found the rubbermaid tub neatly labeled 0-6 months and one by one I pulled out sweet little outfits...teeny tiny outfits that will amazingly look big on you. I dug out the baby detergent from the back of the cabinet, gently washed everything and threw those precious clothes in the dryer. But as I pushed the button and walked away, I was stopped dead in my tracks. There it was. That distantly familiar and yet forgotton sound of all those little baby snaps clinking in the dryer. And in that moment it hit me that you are really coming. You were so close I could almost feel you. I could almost smell you. Precious baby toes. Rocking you to sleep. Magical midnight feedings. So much anticipation. So much to look forward to. It's funny what a bunch of clinking snaps can do.

For some, it's hearing that first heartbeat that makes the surreal experience of pregnancy become real. For others, it's the first kicks and signs of visible belly movements that provide a reality check. For veteran moms, like Deena, it's the sound of tiny clothes snaps clinking their way through the dryer. Whatever it is that makes you realize the moment you've been awaiting is almost here, document it in a special page. Use computer software to create a simple layout that illustrates your trigger, and journal your emotions that come flooding forward.

SNAPS *by Deena Wuest*

Supplies: Image editing software (Adobe); page kit by Leora Sanford (Designer Digitals); dated journal brush, labels, tags by Katie Pertiet (Designer Digitals); torn edges by Anna Aspnes (Designer Digitals); Misc: Avant Garde and Impact fonts

There is nothing more

Exciting than the last few

Months of your first pregnancy

I loved being able to watch you

Wait for your daughter, and see

The differences in how you compared

To me. Your tiny belly, my huge one.

Your lack of morning sickness,

My constant puking. We shared

A lot in our lives, but this is one

Thing I won't soon forget

Anticipating Rebekah.

They say every pregnancy is different, which may be why most mothers love to swap details. Reflect this female-bonding phenomenon by creating a layout of comparison. A vibrant layout such as this is a fun way to unify the differences in pregnancies, be it comparing your own experiences or yours with a loved one's. By juxtaposing images, you tell the tale of two bellies, while journaling strips share the details. Create your own embellishments by stamping images in paint, cutting them out and then setting the pieces on foam adhesive for dimension.

THE WAITING GAME
by Ruth Akers

Supplies: Cardstock; patterned paper, stamps (Paper Salon); letter stickers (American Crafts, Paper Salon); buttons, eyelets (American Crafts); Misc: acrylic paint, adhesive foam, thread

For young children waiting to become older brothers and sisters, the anticipation of a new sibling's arrival can be nearly as intense as the night before Christmas. Cherish the questions and quotes of these older siblings on special layouts all their own, such as Colleen's sentimental design. A sweet photo of mom's belly with the eager siblings serves as a tender reminder of how a child's birth was a family affair.

WHEN? *by Colleen Stearns*

Supplies: Cardstock; patterned paper (BasicGrey, Chatterbox, Heidi Grace); chipboard letters (Chatterbox); chipboard accents (Heidi Grace, Heidi Swapp); journaling tab (Jenni Bowlin); sticker (EK Success); Misc: pen, ink

When will my brother be here?
When can I see him?
When can he play with me?

Forty weeks can seem like an eternity, as with each passing day it becomes more real that you are about to partake in a miracle. Before and after photos captured on one joyful design are a great means to organize emotions, share feelings and celebrate a prize worth the wait. By simply layering blocks of patterned paper in vibrant colors and energetic patterns, Katie was able to express the happiness and excitement over the waiting process, and beautifully emphasized her black-and-white images.

WAITING *by Katie Burnett*

Supplies: Cardstock; patterned paper (BasicGrey, Fancy Pants, Heidi Grace, Junkitz, Martha Stewart, Scenic Route, SEI); bookplates (BasicGrey, Li'l Davis); letter stickers (Doodlebug); rub-ons (7gypsies); brads, chipboard (Junkitz); image editing software (Adobe); photo frame by Rhonna Farrer (Two Peas in a Bucket); clip (Heidi Swapp); Misc: pen

*Wh*ile you're waiting!

You have months of eager anticipation ahead of you, so try scrapping one (or more) of these topics while you wait.

- *Reactions to the news of your pregnancy*
- *Doctor appointments and sonograms*
- *Current events, hit songs, blockbuster movies, popular TV shows, etc.*
- *Prepping the nursery*
- *Choosing baby's name*

- *Discovery of baby's gender*
- *Hopes and dreams for baby*
- *Worries and fears during pregnancy*
- *Details of your pregnancy*
- *Your growing baby belly*

Anusha (Beautiful Morningstar) aka. Nini

PREGNANCY: First, planned
DUE DATE: October 12, 2002
SYMPTOMS: Terrible nausea, Anemia Gestational Diabetes, Pre-term labor
TOTAL WEIGHT GAIN: 8 lbs.
LABOR DURATION: 7 hours
BIRTH PROCESS: Natural child birth, fast dilation, slept thru labor, used Stadol for pain relief, Vaccum Extractor used, 4th Degree episiotomy
BABY ARRIVED: September 26, 2002; 1:59 am
VITAL STATS: 6 lbs.; 19 inches

PREGNANCY: Second, sweet surprise
DUE DATE: May 5, 2005
SYMPTOMS: Occasional nausea, sudden bleeding, hospitalized for passing kidney stones, acute Bronchitis throughout third trimester, several hospitalizations before and after delivery due to a wide array of complications
TOTAL WEIGHT GAIN: 10 lbs
BIRTH PROCESS: Induction planned Emergency C-section, cord around baby's neck.
BABY ARRIVED: April 19, 2005; 11:58 am
VITAL STATS: 7 lbs 0.3 oz; 20 inches

In hindsight, both my pregnancies were difficult. But I enjoyed them both despite all the pain and feel truly blessed to be rewarded so wonderfully.

Ayush (Blessed with a long life) aka. Om

A symmetrical design provides a perfect layout for a page built for two, comparing and contrasting pregnancies and birth experiences. Create a unified look like Mau did here by arranging each baby's photo and journaling horizontally on your page, with each focal feature balanced in opposing corners. A title created with dreamlike, acrylic letters ties the layout together when set vertically down the middle of the page. And sheer flower embellishments lend a visual fragrance as sweet as that new-baby smell.

SWEET *by Mou Saha*

Supplies: Cardstock; plastic letters (KI Memories); clear flowers (Heidi Swapp); epoxy accents (K&Co.); stars (Darice); Misc: Arial Narrow font, paper punch, pen

my gift

unwrapped

2006 was a year of many good changes for our family. We moved from New Mexico to Muncie, IN after David got a job there. We were thrilled to move close to family again. So with our move to a new state and a new house, we were happy to find out that we would be adding a new member to our family as well. What a perfect gift! Abby was born November 29, 2006.

Many of us feel self-conscious about our oversized bellies and we put the nix on any belly shots, much to our scrapbooking dismay. It took Maureen until her fourth pregnancy to take photos of her naked tummy, but as this beautiful digital layout shows, she is so thankful she did! Take photos of yourself using a tripod and camera timer, and then use the magic of image editing software to complete the look. How amazing to look back upon the tiny miracle wrapped up inside you, that soon you will wrap up in your arms.

MY GIFT UNWRAPPED *by Maureen Spell*

Supplies: Image editing software (Adobe); patterned paper by Dana Zarling (Designer Digitals); frame by Katie Pertiet (Designer Digitals); masking tape by Anna Aspnes (Designer Digitals); dot flourish by Kellie Mize (Designer Digitals); Misc: 2Ps Fragile, Century Gothic and You are so Loved fonts

We prayed for a
boy and God
answered with
the sweetest, most
handsome little
guy ever!

someOne
neW
to

love

Lion

chapter

TWO

getting to *know* you

There is a sense of unity found in your baby's first cry, as your little one gasps in amazement for that first breath of air, and you sit back breathless, overwhelmed by more love than you could have ever imagined your heart could handle. And as your eyes meet for that very first time, it's as if you are reconnecting with someone you have always known. In one instant your heart and mind are reprogrammed, and suddenly you can't imagine what your life was ever like before baby. At the sound of your voice or the warmth of your touch, your little one is instantly calmed, knowing that in your care, wrapped in your love, all is right with the world. As you and your little one bond in the weeks and months to follow, savor the memories along the way. Heartfelt scrapbook pages help you to remember in the years ahead how such big love began in such a tiny package.

Those first images of your newborn are treasured memories that deserve pages capturing the emotion of your introduction. Jaime used lively patterned paper accentuated with shimmering circles to repeat the circular theme found in her patterns, foam flowers and die-cut florals, implying emotional cartwheels of joy. Vibrant colors create a captivating energy on the page, while minimal journaling shares the essence of a truly special delivery.

NEW ARRIVAL *by Jaime Warren*

Supplies: Cardstock; patterned paper (Scenic Route); rhinestone accents, title words (Heidi Swapp); foam flowers (American Crafts)

The repetition of shapes can be used to suck you right in to the heart and soul of your images, as Jen demonstrates on this pretty pastel page. The layering of frames, created through matting, photo corners, paints and more pull the eye inward as the frames grow smaller, closing in on the main focus of your photo, as Jen illustrates. An amusing text box, checking off your child's vital statistics and highlighting key words is a fun way to display information with minimal text.

PRECIOUS BABY *by Jen Erickson*

Supplies: Cardstock; patterned paper (7gypsies); chipboard word, photo corners and tabs, ribbon, transparent frame (Heidi Swapp); wooden flower (Li'l Davis); rickrack (Doodlebug); decorative tape (Making Memories); Misc: acrylic paint, ink, pen, staples

3 DAYS OLD

Beautiful

DELIGHT

Looking back at this photo, I still remember exactly how I felt. Just 3 days before, you came into our lives. Just 3 days before, we became new parents. You changed our lives forever that day—for the better. You looked so small and fragile, I just wanted to hold you and protect you from any harm or hurt. Thank you so much for bringing so much love and happiness in our lives.

forever grateful forever grateful

I love you so much then, now and always.

xoxo, Mum
August, 2007

Every baby girl needs a page like this one that dotes on their inner princess. Shirley used baby-soft felt for floral accents and a precious, elegant crown set over the image of her daughter. Rhinestones lend feminine flair and dazzle, while lace and lavish ribbons enhance the look. Try creating your own girly-girl title by painting chipboard letters white and then stamping them in pink with a sweet and swirly pattern.

3 DAYS OLD *by Shirley Chai*

Supplies: Chipboard letters, die-cut shapes, felt, lace, journaling card, patterned paper, ribbon, stamps (Fancy Pants); Misc: acrylic paint, ink, rhinestones, rhinestone brads

To create a page that balances an all-boy look with sweet sentiment, Heather employed subtle stamping and paper with a small print in masculine hues. By keeping your page simple and allowing a colored background to convey the gender of your child, you can easily add textural floral accents in coordinating colors to express the joy of your own sweet miracle. To achieve the effect of subtle stamping in your background, simply pre-stamp your image on scrap paper to remove excess ink.

MIRACLE *by Heather Bowser*

Supplies: Cardstock; patterned paper (7gypsies); letter stickers (KI Memories); flowers
(Prima); stamps (October Afternoon); journaling card (My Mind's Eye); Misc: brads, ink

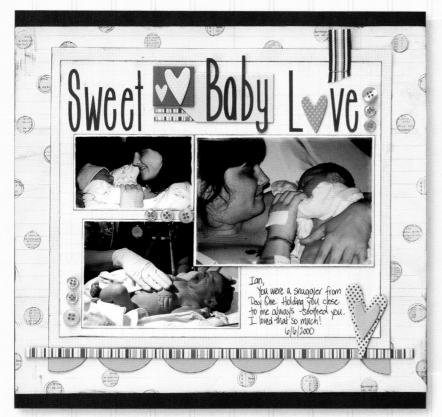

Supplies: Cardstock; patterned paper (Autumn Leaves, Doodlebug, Heidi Grace, Scenic Route); chipboard accents (Heidi Grace); letter stickers (Chatterbox); buttons (Autumn Leaves); ribbon (May Arts); Misc: ink, pen

Baby blue buttons and soft shades of brown give a baby boy look to a page design, while capturing the tenderness of a mother's love. Colleen was able to quiet the look of busy photos by tying them together in a well-balanced arrangement that still makes an emotional impact. Simple journaling and embellishments balance out the busyness of the images. Remember that soft, low-key colors and patterns and sweet embellishments can quiet a page and allude to the comfort of mommy's arms.

SWEET BABY LOVE *by Colleen Stearns*

Amy captured the reward of hard work and sheer strength involved in giving birth on this labor of love, combining two images for an effect that focuses on mother and child. To achieve this look, make two digital copies of your original photo. Using photo editing software, make one photo the size of your layout and blend it into the background. Draw attention to the picture's focal point by placing the cropped version of the photo behind a frame in full-color mode.

STRENGTH *by Amy Knepper*

Supplies: Image editing software (Adobe); blue flower, heart, papers, photo frames, rickrack by Jessica Bolton (Scrapbook Graphics); hand-stamped letters by Michelle Coleman (Second Mile Freebies); paint strokes by Michelle Godin (Scrapbook Graphics); tear by Jen Caputo (Scrapbook Graphics); safety pin tag by Ann DeJong (Funky Playground Designs); word strips by Misty Cato (Scrapbook Elements); Misc: DesertDogHMK and PassionsConflictROB fonts

- You're a big "talker"...always cooing...your doctor is amazed at how many sounds you can make already!

- You love your big brother...always watching him and smiling.

- You weigh over 13 pounds and are gaining fast! You've outgrown most of your 0-3 mos. clothes!

- You still sleep in your carseat due to having reflux.

- You don't lay still for very long...always kicking those feet!

- You're sleeping pretty well at night...from about 9-3 or 4 and then up again at 7. Taking good naps during the day and falling asleep on your own!

Create a snapshot to treasure your cutie's monthly stats on a layout like Kelly's, which features the many faces of her special guy. Choose one favorite photo as the focal point, and then create a strip of animation down the center of the layout. Balance the layout with a journaling block recording baby's facts. When time doesn't permit for hand-stitched accents, create the illusion by bordering your design in pen.

2 MONTHS *by Kelly Noel*

Supplies: Cardstock; patterned paper, round sticker (KI Memories); chipboard letters, number sticker, letter sticker (American Crafts); Misc: SP You've Got Mail font, pen

All about b*a*by!

You have pictures piling up. Now what? If you're stumped for which ones to record, check out these tried-and-true topics for scrapping baby's first year.

Monthly Development Diaries—Try pages with journaling about your infant's monthly physical developments, latest skills and favorite activities.

Milestone Pages—Create specific pages dedicated to baby's major milestones like learning to crawl, first tooth, first haircut and first taste of solid food.

Photo Montage—Pull together highlights from several months into a photo montage.

Baby Love—Design a page around your little one's favorite things, such as pacifiers, stuffed animals, baby slings, rice cereal and more.

A Year at a Glance—Shoot a photo of baby each month with the same photo prop to show how your little one grows during the year.

ABCs of Baby—Have fun coming up with an ABC-themed album, using a letter of the alphabet per page that illustrates elements of baby's life, such as "A is for Angel," "B is for Brother," "C is for Crying," and so forth.

Documenting the details of your darling's month-old birthdays makes for dynamic milestone pages, such as this one. Heather played up the colors from her photo to create an energetic layout, which shares her child's statistics in colorful journaling strips set in a variety of cheerful fonts. Flower accents set about the page create a visual triangle that pulls the eye immediately to the precious photo, while a wave-cut strip does double-duty framing the image and illuminating the title.

3 MONTHS *by Heather Bowser*

Supplies: Cardstock; patterned paper (American Crafts, Scenic Route); letter stickers (American Crafts); die-cut flowers (My Mind's Eye)

Digital layouts explode with embellishments and pizzazz when photo editing software comes out to play. Tania used photo editing software to enhance her photo's colors, and then added digital brushes and funky, fun digital elements in bold colors to express her little one's playful personality.

2 CUTE *by Tania Cordova Shaw*

Supplies: Image editing software (Adobe); papers by Corina Nielsen (Funky Playground); swirl and letter brushes by Shawna Clingerman (Sweet Shoppe); buttons by Jessica Bolton (Scrapbook Graphics) and by Natalie Braxton (Lilypad); labels by Traci Reed (Scrapbook Graphics); ribbon by Lori Barnhurst (Little Dreamer); bulletin board elements (Gina Miller); Mr. Funk kit by Ashley Olsen (Digi Shoppe); Photoshop action (EZ Actions)

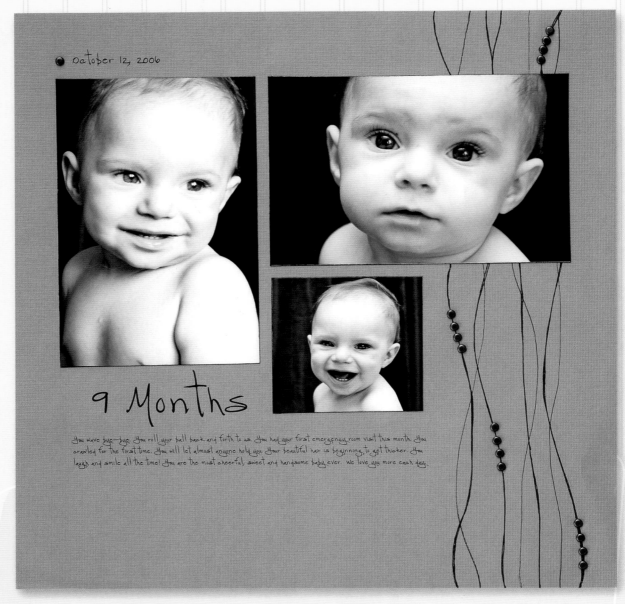

october 12, 2006

9 Months

You wave bye-bye. You roll your ball back and forth to us. You had your first emergency room visit this month. You crawled for the first time. You will let almost anyone hold you. Your beautiful hair is beginning to get thicker. You laugh and smile all the time! You are the most cheerful, sweet and handsome baby ever. We love you more each day.

When wanting to embellish a classic-looking creation with little or no bulk, look to your pen for inspiration. April created this whimsical free fall of wispy lines adorned with little brads, creating the illusion of fibers and beads, sans glue, stress or mess! Add your own freehand elements to fill white space or make a page pop.

9 MONTHS *by April Massad*   Supplies: Cardstock; Misc: CK Jacque font, brads, pen

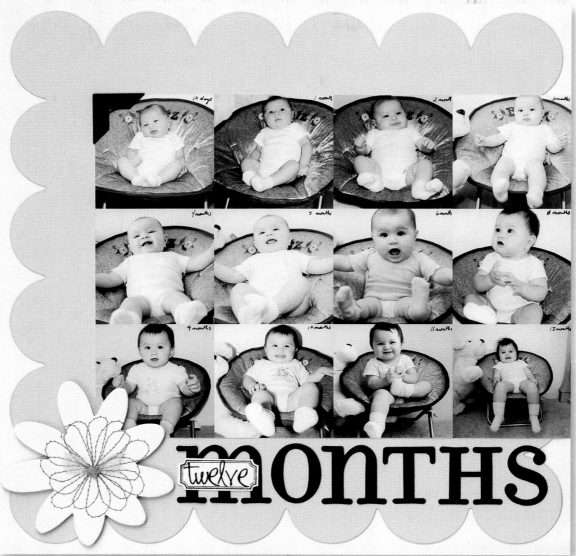

Time flies when you're having fun with baby. You blink and they're all grown up. Look back at a year in slow-mo by creating a monthly collage, like Athena's. A great way to see the distinct changes in your little one is to take a monthly photo using the same object, such as a chair, in each picture. To easily size and fit all your photos on a page, arrange them in a photo editing program and print them as one sheet.

TWELVE MONTHS *by Athena Mejia*

Supplies: Cardstock; letter stickers, rub-on letters (Making Memories); ribbon (Heidi Swapp); rub-on flower (Autumn Leaves); die-cut shape (QuicKutz); Misc: ink, pen, velvet paper

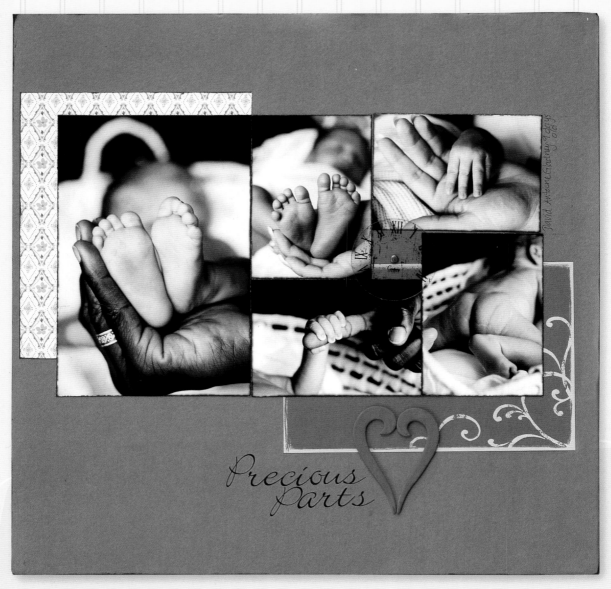

Preserving baby images using a classic or vintage look will always ensure a layout with style. Melissa began this timeless tribute to her little one's features by creating an arrangement of sepia-toned and black-and-white photos. She carried the look throughout the page with subtly patterned paper and slightly distressed acetate embellishments. A chipboard heart adds textural elegance, while mimicking the delicate flow of a fabulous font and flourish.

PRECIOUS PARTS *by Melissa Kelley*

Supplies: Cardstock; patterned paper (Chatterbox); rub-on letters (Making Memories); transparent frame (My Mind's Eye); clock accent (Heidi Swapp); chipboard shapes (Fancy Pants); Misc: brad, ink, paint

Baby feet are simply irresistible, and close-ups of your little one's ten tiny toes are images that deserve a page all their own, as Heather shows here. A close-up image serving as a focal point photo immediately draws in the eye, while a similar image repeated as an accent provides a sense of movement across the page. A fun way to recognize which child's feet you're drooling over is to include a number line, as Heather did using colorful brads to indicate that these fabulous feet belong to her baby number nine!

SWEET DREAMS *by Heather Bowser*

Supplies: Cardstock; patterned paper (Cosmo Cricket); chipboard letters (American Crafts); number and accent stickers (7gypsies); stamp (October Afternoon); Misc: brad, flower, ink

Who can resist the power of those precious baby feet? Kelly used her daughter's tiny toes as the underlying theme of this layout which highlights her top ten loves about her little one. Use a black marker to draw attention to the details of your black-and-white images, as Kelly demonstrates here by highlighting the tiny toes. Also try using embellishments to mimic a detail in your photo, like Kelly did repeating the roundness of baby's toes through ten ribbon loops bordering the page.

PERFECT 10 *by Kelly O'Dell*

Supplies: Photo quality paper; patterned paper (Chatterbox); image editing software (Adobe); Misc: Garamond and Pea Amy Rica Script fonts, clip, marker, ribbon

true baby blues

who knew they'd be so blue?

Hey Jones! Where d'ya get those pretty blue eyes? Your sisters and I have brown and your dad has green. O well I love them because they are yours and they match your sparkling smile.

Capture the same twinkle found in your little one's gleaming eyes on pages that shimmer, like Lana's. To play up the brilliant blue of her babe's pretty peepers, Lana set a cropped enlarged color photo between similar black-and-white accent shots. Use sparkling gems to emphasize your theme, setting printed swirls in motion or embellishing other accents with bling. Repetition of a thematic element like stars unifies the page while pulling the eye throughout the design.

WHO KNEW THEY'D BE SO BLUE?
by Lana Rappette

Supplies: Cardstock; patterned paper (Daisy Bucket, KI Memories); foam star (American Crafts); rhinestone brads, ribbon (Making Memories); doodle template (Crafter's Workshop); stamp (Autumn Leaves); digital swirls by Rhonna Farrer (Two Peas in a Bucket); Misc: Cinta and Tekton Pro fonts, ink, pen

LOVE

In your eyes

when i see you

I can see it in your eyes, that certain **something**...

Since the moment we first met, I have **always** felt that you looked at me with so much **love** and such an amazing **connection**.

I truly believe that you have an *old soul.*

The way your eyes **SPARKLE** when you smile. The **pride** you express when I cheer for you after you've done something new.

How you try to win me over with those **puppy dog** *eyes*.

And, oh boy, how you speak to me with your eyes when you are *crying*.

You seem *wise* beyond your years, seem able to gather so much from observing.

It's said that the eyes are the **WINDOW** to the **SOUL**. I believe that to be true every time I look into your *beautiful eyes*.

Cherish the details of your little one on an innocent and sweet two-page spread, like Stacey's. A close-up of your favorite feature—like big eyes or tiny toes—can be swaddled sweetly in decorative papers. Offset the details with a bold title font. Then use the highlighted feature as the focus of your journaling, sharing your thoughts in different sizes and fonts to accentuate thematic words for emphasis.

IN YOUR EYES *by Stacey Michaud*

Supplies: Cardstock; buttons, chipboard letters, patterned paper, ribbon (Making Memories); word stickers (Colorbok, EK Success); chipboard tag, rub-on (Colorbok); chipboard flower (Jo-Ann); flower (Prima); Misc: brads, ink, transparent label

A baby's little belly is a precious sight, and Michelle has fun with her son's terrific tummy. This page design is filled with circular elements, such as the decorative overlay, flowers, brads and the letter "b," all which help emphasize the round baby belly in the photo. This page also inspires us to think of new ways to use traditional accents, such as folding flowers in half to add whimsy to photos.

LI'L BUDDHA BELLY *by Michelle Gowland*

Supplies: Cardstock; patterned paper (Die Cuts With A View, take-out bag); transparency (Hambly); flower (Bazzill, Prima); die-cut letters and shapes (Provo Craft); Misc: brads, ink, pens

There are few things more endearing than a sleeping baby. Capture close-up images of your own sleeping beauty and create a peaceful page around one photo like Amy did. A single black-and-white image emphasizes the timeless look of contentment and peace, while quiet ribbons and tags adorned with bows lend the layout soft texture and dimension. Try tucking your focal photo snugly in place by framing the image in soothing shades of subtly patterned papers.

SHHH *by Amy Williams*

I captured this picture while you were sleeping on your daddy's chest. When you are awake you are so alert and always smiling. Your arms and legs are in constant motion. I love playing with you and discovering your personality. But there is something about a sleeping baby. So very content... So very precious!

Supplies: Cardstock; patterned paper (Chatterbox); tag rim (Making Memories); oval accent, rub-on letters (Heidi Swapp); ribbon (American Crafts, May Arts); Misc: brads, pen

It's difficult not to wonder what babies dream about, as they lay there fast asleep in blissful slumber. Sleepy time layouts provide the perfect opportunities to design a look around a favorite lullaby or song lyrics. The look of swirls and flourishes lends gently flowing movement to a page, drifting over the background in sweet serenity. Melissa added texture to her whispery waves by first tracing the designs in pencil then running them through her sewing machine. This provided the perfectly spaced holes she needed to embroider curls of contentment with a simple backstitch.

WHEN YOU DREAM *by Melissa Kelley*

when you dream, what do you dream about?
when you dream, what do you dream about?
are they colour or black and white,
yiddish or english or languages
not yet conceived?
are they silent or boisterous?
do you hear noises just
loud enough to be perceived? do you hear del
Shannon's "runaway" playing on
transistor radio waves?
with so little experience, your mind
not yet cognizant
are you wise beyond your few days? when you dream,
what do you dream about? when you dream

When you dream

Supplies: Patterned paper (Chatterbox, Creative Imaginations, My Mind's Eye); letter stickers (Creative Imaginations); flowers (Prima); buttons (Doodlebug); conchos, stickers (Scrapworks); Misc: Snowshoe font, floss, transparency

Wishes come true on this enchanting layout of bold contrasts, crisp lines and dynamic arrangement. For journaling you want to keep hidden, or as a means of saving space, follow Sue's example by tucking a journaling tag behind the focal point photo. To add visual interest, use a ruler to line up and tear diagonal edges of one side of your page arrangement, balancing out a bold and beautiful vertical title block.

I WISH *by Sue Kristoff*

Supplies: Patterned paper, letter stickers (BasicGrey); chip-board heart and letters (Making Memories); clock accent (Heidi Swapp); Misc: brad, pen

... that you always have reason to smile.
... that you stay healthy and grow up strong.
... that you find your soulmate (and have some grandchildren!)
... that you discover your talents and share them with the world.
... that I would live long enough to watch you grow and thrive.

The world awaits your little one to explore it. Document the sense of wonder sure to be found as your baby steps out to discover his surroundings. Heather played up the negative space in her layout to mimic the look of a big, wide world found in her oversized photo. To keep a layout simple, try highlighting just one element, such as the stripes in a shirt. Here, Heather repeated stripes in a simple yet playful border.

DREAM BIG *by Heather Bowser*

Supplies: Cardstock; patterned paper (Three Bugs in a Rug); chipboard letters (American Crafts); stamp (October Afternoon); Misc: ink, pen

The times a child plays independently are treasured moments for Mom, and call for a page of peace and tranquility like Leah's. A great way to obtain that soft, serene setting is to choose an embossed paper in calming colors. And keep in mind that baby pages don't always require "baby" patterns. Leah's sophisticated, floral pattern provides texture, movement and visual interest and evokes an appropriate feeling of calm and quiet.

A QUIET MOMENT
by Leah Farquharson

Supplies: Patterned paper (K&Co., Scenic Route); chipboard letters (American Crafts); sticker accents (7gypsies, Martha Stewart); Misc: acrylic paint, chalk, pen

For most babies, a simple smile at them is all it takes to get a smile back. Not for Samantha. To get a smile from her, it's going to take some serious effort on the part of the person wanting the smile. First, Sam has to know you. If she doesn't, it's very doubtful that you'll get more than a questioning look out of this little gal. Secondly, a little tickle under the arm helps but is not a guarantee. And lastly, she just plain has to be in the mood. If you're Mommy or Daddy, as long as there's no camera in your face, the rules don't apply & she's a little sunbeam. But let me tell you, if you can do the work & get her to smile, it's worth the effort. Think she's pretty now? Her smile will knock you over.

seriouʒly

crack a smile, girl

Easter 2007

Many children love to ham it up in front of the camera, while others indignantly protest their parental paparazzi. Have fun with your own child's serious, shy or stubborn personality on honest pages like Sheila's. Keep the look lighthearted by using computer software to add a whimsical wave down the middle of your layout, using it to serve as a guide for your journaling. Visual surprises, like the backward "s" in Sheila's title, add to the humor of your little one's protests and make for good laughs in the years ahead.

SERIOUSLY *by Sheila Doherty*

Supplies: Cardstock; patterned paper (Around the Block, My Mind's Eye); die-cut shapes and letters (QuicKutz); date stamps (Technique Tuesday); image editing software (Adobe); Misc: Century Gothic font, ink, pen

April gave a timeless quality to her adorable page, setting a black-and-white photo against a neutral background and adding a bit of color with embellishments. You can easily replicate April's heart embellishment. Start by tracing around a heart-shaped rub-on (like this word-filled heart) on a small piece of cardstock; trace about ¼" (6mm) larger than the size of the rub-on. Cut strips of patterned paper and adhere them to the cardstock heart. Then apply the rub-on on top of your patterned paper heart.

I LOVE THAT FACE *by April Massad*

Supplies: Cardstock; patterned paper, stickers (My Mind's Eye); rub-ons (Heidi Swapp, Making Memories); brads, stamps (Making Memories); ribbon (American Crafts, Making Memories); Misc: ink, pen

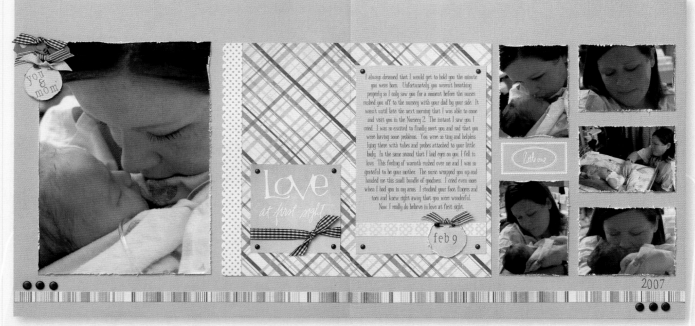

How do you fit all the photos that tell a story on one layout? Amy solved this dilemma by creating a two-page spread. An oversized focal point photo stands alone, while setting the stage for a second page of complementary photos and journaling. A simple patterned band that runs the length of both pages unifies the look, and can be created easily by cutting a wide border sticker in half, using one piece on each page.

LOVE AT FIRST SIGHT *by Amy Williams*

Supplies: Cardstock; patterned paper (BasicGrey); letter stickers (Adornit); rub-ons (Daisy D's); stamps (Autumn Leaves); heart brads (Paper Studio); Misc: CK Anecdote font, ink

LOVE

SWEET

I love these pictures of you Tucker

Your sweet face and expressions

How happy you are just playing

I melt inside. 9 months old

Babies make the funniest faces as they grow, and capturing their animated expressions on a layout is a perfect way to keep your heart smiling long after the chubby cheeks have disappeared. Black-and-white images keep the focus on your child's expressions without distraction, while cheerful patterned papers set a lively, happy tone. Simple journal strips provide a balancing contrast against polka-dot prints, which can be easily enhanced by adding brads for playful dimension.

LOVE SO SWEET *by Heather Bowser*

Supplies: Cardstock; patterned paper (BasicGrey, Making Memories); brads, letter stickers (Making Memories); stamp (October Afternoon); rhinestone stickers (Heidi Swapp); Misc: Fancy Free font, bookplate, ink, pen

EVERY DAY

I ♥ you
more

The more we grow to know our babies, the more deeply we seem to fall in love over and over again. For this love that seems to have no words, often a single image of your child's face will say it all. Heather pulled off a simple, yet powerful piece by combining a few coordinating patterns on a plain cardstock background. Punched patterned paper circles create a large, scallop border that emphasizes the shape of her title embellishment. The hand-drawn designs create a whimsical border and lend a loving touch to negative space needing a hint of pizzazz.

EVERY DAY I LOVE YOU MORE *by Heather Bowser*   *Supplies: Cardstock; chipboard shapes, patterned paper (Imagination Project); chipboard letters and heart (Heidi Swapp); Misc: pen*

A vintage page takes on a fresh 'tude, when modern color combos, felt accents and aesthetic surprises collide in a creation of love. Cindy cut away the upper right portion of this adorable page at the same angle as her focal point photo, and then filled the space with a strip of scalloped paper. Try framing your precious black-and-white photos in vibrant accents, like this golden heart, to add extra oomph.

SOMEONE NEW TO LOVE
by Cindy Tobey

Supplies: Patterned paper (Creative Imaginations, Fancy Pants); letter stickers (Making Memories); chipboard, felt shapes, lace, ribbon (Fancy Pants); buttons (Autumn Leaves); decorative tape (Heidi Swapp); brads (KI Memories, Queen & Co.); rub-on bird (Hambly); Misc: acrylic paint, floss, ink, pen, staples

Convey loads of love with lots of hearts. And for a look that says comfort, use textured accents such as rickrack, buttons and hand stitching. Try taking your page dimension to the next level, as Maegan did here, by placing tissue paper under a cut heart and stitching around it to make a soft, pillow-like embellishment.

WE WILL ALWAYS LOVE YOU *by Maegan Hall*

Supplies: Kraft cardstock; patterned paper (KI Memories); brads, rickrack (Doodlebug); buttons (Autumn Leaves, Doodlebug, Making Memories); photo corners (Heidi Swapp); Misc: French Script font, decorative scissors, floss

♥ MYBABYBOY

THIS PHOTO OF YOU JUST SINGS A LOVE SONG TO MY HEART

Sometimes a single look from a little one is all it takes to melt our hearts into a puddle of goo. For pages that preserve those golden glimpses, a clean, uncluttered look works well. To create this modern design, Mindy used a bold, graphic font for her title, weaving her single-line journaling into the title block. A single chipboard accent lends a subtle texture and depth to the page, and color pulls the layout together.

MY BABY BOY *by Mindy Bush*

Supplies: Cardstock; patterned paper (A2Z, BasicGrey); chipboard heart (Heidi Swapp); Misc: MLB Astros font

Even square pages can incorporate soft edges. Circles are perfect for dressing up pages with big round eyes and pink chubby cheeks. To round out her layout, Lisa simply layered a large paper circle over her background cardstock sheet. She played up the curves with a large "p," a circular journaling space and round embellishments.

PINK *by Lisa Tutman-Oglesby*

Supplies: Cardstock; patterned paper (Daisy D's, Making Memories); chipboard letters (Zsiage); flowers (Chatterbox, Doodlebug, EK Success, Making Memories, My Mind's Eye, Prima); buttons (Autumn Leaves); chipboard heart, rhinestones (Heidi Swapp); journaling accent (Daisy D's); metal frame (Making Memories); photo corner (Colorbok); rub-on (American Crafts); Misc: acrylic paint, thread

A first tooth is big news for baby, and deserves a milestone memory page like Athena's. Papers and accents in a pink hue echo the look of baby's gums, and when offset by a pearly white button, like on the flower embellishment, dimension breaks right through.

FIRST CUT *by Athena Mejia*

Supplies: Cardstock; patterned paper (Chatterbox); chipboard letters (Scenic Route); die-cut letters and shapes (QuickKutz); flower (Li'l Davis); stamps (Autumn Leaves, Stampin' Up); Misc: brads, button, ink, pen, thread

Nothing quite says "sweet baby girl" like flowers do, as Samantha's endearing floral framework shows. Make your own border bouquet by assembling paper flowers in layers of coordinating colors. Use rickrack to embrace journaling and lend a soft, flowing texture that balances a scripted title in the same color. Include small images of your little one's tiny features in layouts featuring close-up shots. And use a grown-up hand to illustrate just how small your baby's hand is.

BLESSING DAY *by Samantha Walker*

Supplies: Cardstock; patterned paper (Chatterbox, KI Memories); die-cut letters (Sizzix); rickrack (SEI); flowers (Prima); brads (Making Memories); Misc: corner rounder, ink, pen

Along the same lines as crawling and walking, your child's first haircut ranks high among milestones for memory pages. A striped patterned paper, such as the one Andrea chose, is a fun way to set the tone with a look reminiscent of old-fashioned barbershop poles. Document the details of the event in an innovative way, such as incorporating stamped words in your journaling block and using colorful letter stickers to emphasize phrases. And of course, don't forget to include that first lock of cut hair in a transparent envelope.

HAIRCUT *by Andrea Friebus*   *Supplies: Cardstock; patterned paper (SEI); flower (All My Memories); envelope (3L); date stamp (Costco); Misc: brads, ink, letter stamps, pen*

Beyond baby phot_os!

Making lovable layouts doesn't have to stop with photos. Try adding memorabilia like these:

- *Birth certificate*
- *Birth announcement card*
- *Baby shower invitation*
- *Cards sent by family and friends*
- *Hospital bracelets*

- *Labels from favorite baby food jars*
- *Clothing tags or labels*
- *Footprints and handprints*
- *Newspaper announcement*
- *Lock of hair*

Savor the short time span of infancy on an irresistible layout, like Marci's, which showcases adorable photos on a simple layout. To keep the page's look cohesive, arrange images with the same backdrop together and round the corners of the collective whole. Pull the design together by stamping over your focal point photo with a decorative flourish. Polish off the piece with a powerful title created by hovering decorative chipboard letters over the photos using adhesive foam.

ADORE *by Marci Lambert*

Supplies: Cardstock; patterned paper (BasicGrey); die-cut letters (Daisy D's); letter sticker (K&Co.); stamps (EK Success, Hobby Lobby, Technique Tuesday); rub-on (American Crafts); Misc: adhesive foam, circle punch, ink

Precious pages need not be filled with frills. Sometimes using a singular symbol, such as the heart on Jaime's love-filled layout, to carry out a theme conveys a stronger sentiment than lots of embellishment. Using various styles and sizes of a single object highlights the heart of a page.

MY HEART *by Jaime Warren*

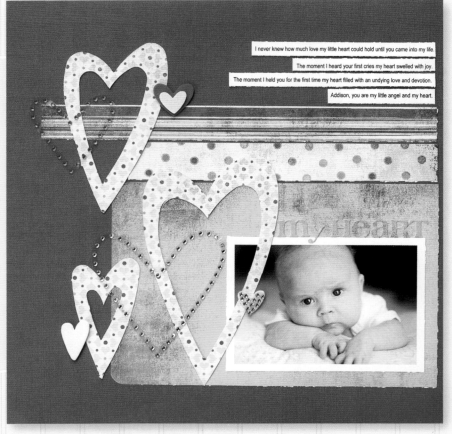

Supplies: Cardstock; letter stickers, patterned paper (BasicGrey); foam hearts (American Crafts); rhinestone hearts (Heidi Swapp); die-cut heart (Provo Craft)

Only a parent knows her child intimately by each detailed nook and cranny, from the top of the baby's head to the tips of tiny toes. To design a page that shows separate pictures in a cohesive whole, consider an arrangement such as Ruth's. Use photo editing software to print your photos in a unified tone. Then create a simple accent piece with coordinating ephemera to tie the images together. After arranging both large and little letters in a variety of textures over a briskly painted background, use stamps all along the title area with sweetly flowing words.

I ALREADY KNOW YOU *by Ruth Akers*

Supplies: Cardstock; chipboard letters, letter stickers, patterned paper, stamps (Paper Salon); brads, chipboard hearts, eyelets, ribbon, rub-ons (American Crafts); Misc: button, paint, safety pin, tag, thread

Help your child's smile radiate off the page with a layout that simply shines, like Jennifer's. To create this fun, shimmery title, trace chipboard letters onto a plain transparency and cut around the letters, coloring the backs with a permanent marker. Glue the front side of the chipboard letters to tinfoil and cut around them. Finish the look by gluing the colored transparency letters over the foil letters. Complement your shining letters by adding coordinating ribbon with just a bit of sheen.

SHINE *by Jennifer Armentrout*

Supplies: *Cardstock; patterned paper (Hambly, Lazar); transparency (Hambly); chipboard letters (American Crafts); ribbon (Michaels); Misc: pen, tinfoil, transparency*

Choosing a color scheme can be super simple by taking the hues right from your photos. Sherry wanted to create a layout that looked as yummy and juicy as the watermelon in her photos, and achieved that effect through her vibrant color scheme. Her choice of hot pink and green complements the watermelon theme perfectly, creating a bright and cheerful summer page.

WATERMELON *by Sherry Wright*

Supplies: *Patterned paper, rub-ons (Fancy Pants); letter stickers (American Crafts); chipboard and acrylic letters (Heidi Swapp); felt (Queen & Co.); journaling accent (Autumn Leaves); ribbon (Offray); Misc: buttons, ink*

Baby's first playmates are often of the stuffed or plastic variety, but loved with reckless abandon nonetheless. Cherish the images of your baby hard at play on fun-filled pages like Sheila's. Sheila incorporated her title, photo and stamped journaling notes into a free-flowing, organic array of joy. Try creating a collage of playful elements, weaving in a variety of simple embellishments, such as a heart made from buttons.

BABY LOVE *by Sheila Doherty*

Supplies: Patterned paper (My Mind's Eye); chipboard letters (American Crafts, Cosmo Cricket); metal plates (American Crafts); chipboard arrows, journaling notes, photo corner (Heidi Swapp); buttons (American Crafts, Making Memories); ribbon (KI Memories, Offray); metal frame (Making Memories); stamps (Autumn Leaves, Fontwerks); Misc: decorative paper cutter, floss, ink, pen

Baby GeaR

Do you know anyone who can walk past cute baby stuff and not take a second look? Or not pick it up? I have to say, I'm a sucker for adorable baby goods, especially when it's pink. Go ahead, it's OK, to admit it. Isn't that one of the fun things about shopping for a baby girl? I'd say so. And now that I have a baby daughter of my own, I can now shop for myself... Uh, I meant to say now I can shop for her. You get the picture. I love having a girl and I love all her yummy baby gear. (Spring 07)

Half the fun of a new baby are miniature items you suddenly find in your home. Teeny tiny Mary Jane's, fluffy toy bears, and of course dainty booties—these are a few of any new mom's favorite things, so why not design a layout around the fun of it all? Here, Lisa adds a sentimental touch by cradling the tiny pink footwear in her hands, forming the shape of a heart in her photo.

BABY GEAR *by Lisa Tutman-Oglesby*

Supplies: Cardstock; patterned paper (Chatterbox); chipboard letters (BasicGrey); rhinestones (Heidi Swapp); Misc: acrylic paint, brads, transparency

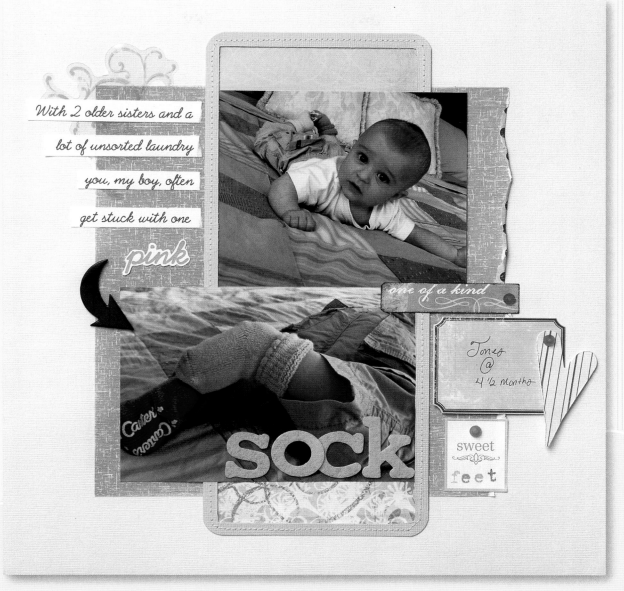

With 2 older sisters and a lot of unsorted laundry you, my boy, often get stuck with one

pink

one of a kind

sock

Jones @ 4 ½ months

sweet feet

Some of the funniest layouts are often about the tiny details of life, such as everyday busyness leading to mismatched socks. Be sure to document these little things to make for big smiles. Lana tailored her title to the layout's theme, using fuzzy blue letter stickers to mimic the texture of socks. To add texture and dimension without a lot of bulk, Lana manipulated paper edges to make them roll and added stitches and distressed edges.

PINK SOCK *by Lana Rappette*

Supplies: Cardstock; patterned paper (Autumn Leaves, Daisy Bucket); letter stickers (American Crafts); arrow brad (Around the Block); transparency (My Mind's Eye); tags (Daisy D's, Heidi Grace); letter stamps (EK Success); Misc: Arizona font, fasteners, ink, pen

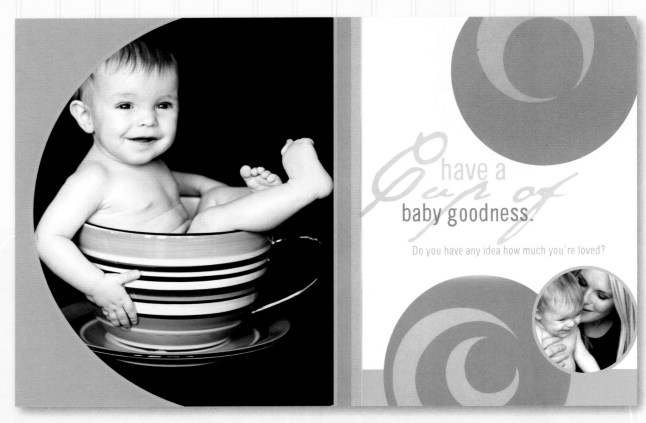

have a Cup of baby goodness.

Do you have any idea how much you're loved?

A playful prop and your favorite baby make for sweet and silly page designs that are sure to leave a smile. Mindy chose a cup and saucer prop to play up a whimsical theme on this graphic design. Colorful circles with inlaid swirls mimic the round cup-o'-joe feel, while a brightly trimmed accent photo completes the look.

CUP OF GOODNESS *by Mindy Bush*   *Supplies: Image editing software*

YEP. You are FUNNY.

Ethan... Even at 11 months, we can already tell you are one funny kid. Like father, like son! 7/04

Children love to make their parents smile, and even at the youngest ages they begin pulling out all the stops to crack us up! Highlight images of your young comedian on sassy, simple layouts like Courtney's. Bold colors create an energizing effect on your page, especially when tied to your photo. You can use hand stitching to lend a homespun feel to your design, and create innovative text boxes that make the page fun.

FUNNY *by Courtney Walsh*

Supplies: Cardstock; letter stickers (Chatterbox, Doodle-bug); brads (Queen & Co.); Misc: floss, pen

MY sWEet
sAssY SuPEr
sPUNKY gIRL At
OnLY 6.5 moNThS
oLd SHE waS AlReaDy
fuLL oF PERSonaliTY

PHOTOS: JuLY 04

Spunky BABY

When designing a bold, energetic layout that conveys your baby's exuberance, try converting photos to black and white for contrast and to keep the page from becoming too busy. Shirley created this fun tribute to her daughter's playful personality, using vibrant flower accents, scalloped journaling strips and elegant rub-ons in cheerful colors. Then she added childlike charm by accenting sophisticated rub-on designs with sassy and sweet brads.

SPUNKY BABY *by Shirley Chai*

Supplies: Patterned paper (KI Memories, Li'l Davis, My Mind's Eye); chipboard letters (Li'l Davis, Queen & Co.); letter stickers (EK Success); brads, charms, flowers (Queen & Co.); rub-ons (Hambly); paper trims (Doodlebug)

How quickly our bundle of joy's personality emerges, be it a laid-back attitude or a fiery temper that flares at will. Layouts, such as Jaime's, are a great way to document the first glimpses of your baby's true colors. Light, airy color schemes keep the look baby soft, while foam flowers and buttons lend childlike dimension with whimsy. Black-and-white photos are a powerful way to emphasize the expressions of your little man or mini diva, while playing up his or her attitude.

FED UP! *by Jaime Warren*

Supplies: Cardstock; patterned paper (BasicGrey); flowers, letter stickers (American Crafts); Misc: buttons

For a simple way to play up your baby's personality, try doodling your own background personalized to the temperament of your child. Lori used colored pencils on white cardstock to create this visual treat of femininity and childhood fantasy that celebrates her little girl's cheerfulness. Incorporate sentimental phrases into your own design, such as nicknames for your little one or words that draw upon the baby's character.

HAPPY BABY *by Lori DiAnni*

Supplies: Cardstock; colored pencils (EK Success); Misc: pen

fresh & clean

Look at you, so fresh and so clean, straight out of the bath.

I love to snuggle your neck and just smell that wonderful baby smell you have.

You always seem so much calmer after a nice warm bath which is wonderful for us both!

Rub-a-dub-dub, it's your babe in the tub! Savor the precious moments of your child's first splashes on squeaky clean layouts that bubble over with carefree charm. The use of a stark white background exudes an air of cleanliness and illustrates the innocence of infancy. A layered arrangement of patterned paper circles in a variety of sizes, along with shimmering rings of bling, create the look of bubbles. Blue patterned paper mimics water as a perfect backdrop for your child's bath-time photo.

FRESH AND CLEAN *by Jaime Warren*   *Supplies: Cardstock; patterned paper (BasicGrey); letter stickers (Doodlebug); rhinestone circles (Heidi Swapp); Misc: circle cutter*

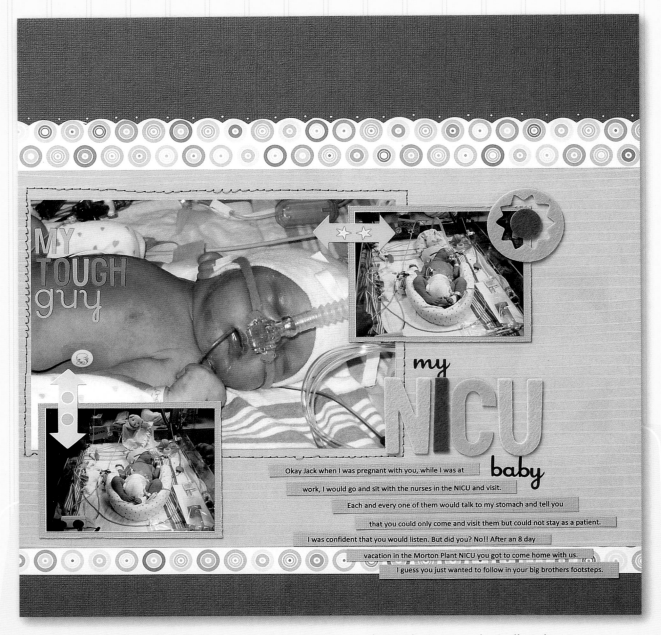

MY TOUGH guy

my NICU baby

Okay Jack when I was pregnant with you, while I was at

work, I would go and sit with the nurses in the NICU and visit.

Each and every one of them would talk to my stomach and tell you

that you could only come and visit them but could not stay as a patient.

I was confident that you would listen. But did you? No!! After an 8 day

vacation in the Morton Plant NICU you got to come home with us.

I guess you just wanted to follow in your big brothers footsteps.

Teeny tough guys deserve visually strong pages to commemorate hospital stints in style. Scalloped scissors are a great way to lighten the look of a serious page and provide movement and a border as well. Plus, if you choose the right size, decorative scissors make cutting out a pattern, as Christine did with this circle paper, a snap.

MY NICU BABY *by Christine Pfeiffer*

Supplies: Cardstock; felt stickers, patterned paper, sticker accents (KI Memories); rub-ons (American Crafts, KI Memories); Misc: pen, thread

Brodey you are my little January Baby! We will always start the new year off celebrating your birthday! You were born almost four weeks early on January 12, 2006. After staying in the hospital for five days we had to bundle you up and take you home! It was so very cold outside! One year later is was even colder! It was so cold that your first birthday plans were foiled by snowstorm after snowstorm! That's bound to happen when you are a January Baby, but you will have many more cold birthdays to come! I love you my little January Baby!

January 12 2006

January 12 2007

A mother's touch of hand stitching provides warmth and texture to a page. Butterfly flourishes like these help welcome a little one home. Weave a page's design together with your title, as April did, by wrapping portions of chipboard title letters with coordinating embroidery floss.

JANUARY BABY by April Massad

Supplies: Cardstock; chipboard letters (Fancy Pants); letter stickers, patterned paper (KI Memories); date stamp (Heidi Swapp); border stamp (Technique Tuesday); Misc: CK Journaling font, floss, ink, pen

Lend your favorite images of baby a whimsical timeless touch by incorporating them into a folk-art style motif, like Lana's. Use round decorative objects, such as circular rub-on quotes, to serve as treetops, while scalloped edge scissors can easily add rolling hills. To accentuate a quiet title, outline the letters in an opaque yellow pen for just enough definition to make them glow.

GOOD THINGS
by Lana Rappette

Supplies: Cardstock; patterned paper (Daisy D's, Fancy Pants, Kodomo); chipboard, letter stickers (Making Memories); rub-ons (Autumn Leaves, Creative Imaginations); heart brad (Around the Block); Misc: decorative scissors, pen, sequins

Time's up!

So many pictures, so little time. Try these time-saving tips for making pages in a snap.

- *Print (or get printed) digital photos* weekly or monthly so they're ready to go when you're ready to scrap.

- *Buy self-adhesive embellishments* for quickly attaching elements.

- *Create a "baby's monthly stats"* template on your computer and print out several copies. Fill in the templates when you have time and use them as journaling for pages.

- *Use prepackaged kits* that include coordinated paper and embellishments.

- *Use big embellishments* like large foam stamp images, oversized letters and big, bold flowers. They'll dress your page more quickly than adding lots of tiny elements.

- *Handwrite your journal entries* and other words on a page. You'll save time on printing, stamping individual letters, or cutting out rub-ons.

A single black-and-white silhouette of a baby's chubby cheeks makes a dynamic impact on a page when set against vibrant colors and patterns. Try a combination of both digital and traditional elements, such as digital papers paired with silk flowers and jewels, as Andrea demonstrates here.

A GIFT FROM GOD *by Andrea Wiebe*

Supplies: Cardstock; letter stamps (Tin Box); buttons (Autumn Leaves, Doodlebug, My Mind's Eye); flower (Imaginisce); Misc: floss, ink, pen, rhinestone; image editing software (Adobe); digital Kraft paper, tag by Gina Cabrera (Digital Design Essentials); patterned paper by Rhonna Farrer (Two Peas in a Bucket); tape by Kate Hadfield (Lilypad)

Try adding the unique look of Lisa's layout to your own page of gratitude by creating a canvas photo frame. Simply print your photo onto inkjet canvas, and cut out the photo, leaving a wide border around it. Snip the border into strips and stamp the strips with baby-themed prints. Fold over the strips and attach buttons or brads.

BLESSING *by Lisa Hoel*

Supplies: Patterned paper (Die Cuts With A View, We R Memory Keepers); chipboard letters (Making Memories); rub-ons (BasicGrey, Melissa Frances); tags (We R Memory Keepers); stamps (Sugarloaf); die-cut shapes (Provo Craft); Misc: adhesive foam, brad, ink, vintage buttons and lace

I know these days will go quickly. As much as I want you to stay tiny for just a little while longer, you are growing and changing every day. These tiny feet will soon be walking and running. These tiny hands will be waving goodbye. And these little legs will be jumping up and down. I look forward to all of your milestones, but hope that I always remember the tiny miracle you were when you came into this world

REMEMBER *you*

With all those cheery colors and cute baby accents, photos can sometimes get lost on a page. To avoid your photos losing focus, convert color photos to black and white, and then add digital frames to the images before printing. The frames provide just enough contrast to help your prints pop on the page. Plus black-and-white photos ensure a timeless look.

REMEMBER YOU *by Greta Hammond*

Supplies: Cardstock; chipboard letters and shapes, patterned paper, rub-ons (Imagination Project); ribbon (Prima); digital frame by Rhonna Farrer (Two Peas in a Bucket); Misc: Bradley Hand font, ink

To celebrate how your infant blooms before your very eyes, a fabulous floral display, like Debbie's, is a sweet way to capture every adorable, serious and silly expression. Create your own flower accents by layering flowers cut from patterned paper and attaching with a colorful brad. Rickrack and painted chipboard swirls create whimsical flower stems for a lively design.

BLOOM & GROW
by Debbie Standard

Supplies: Cardstock; patterned paper (SEI); letter stickers (American Crafts, Doodlebug); chipboard (Fancy Pants); clip (Making Memories); ribbon (American Crafts, unknown); Misc: brads, decorative scissors

Can't find the perfect embellishment to express the emotion of your page? Create your own! Find new uses for everyday accents, such as creating a border by arranging petals cut from silk flowers in a highly textural display. Can't find a patterned paper to complete the look? Digitally design one! Shannon created this blue and pink bubble pattern, which echoes other elements on her page and creates a sense of motion, perfect for a layout about unending growth.

AND STILL SHE GROWS *by Shannon Taylor*

Supplies: Patterned paper (unknown); clock overlay (Heidi Swapp); letter stickers (American Crafts); fabric button (Bazzill); flower petals (Michaels); digital paper (artist's own design); Misc: Frappachino font, floss

dig that CRAZY ★ hair!

cute

Everyone loves Jon's hair. I get comments every time we go out. They laugh & think his hair is the funniest thing ever. This morning a lady wanted to touch it & last week the grocery checker asked to take his photo with her cell phone because she thought he was so cute! I know he really needs his first haircut, but I just love his wild & crazy hair!

AUG 1 3 2007

chapter

THREE

tricks *and* quirks

Once you swaddled your tiny bundle of joy in the folds of a baby soft blanket. Now, your tiny tot wobbles on unsure legs about your household, with baby soft blanket in tow. And as your little one's physical abilities advance, so too will his or her personality, sense of ingenuity and expressions of creativity. Your competitive child will use blankie for a game of tug-of-war. Your mother-hen-in-training will wrap up dollies in love. Your one-of-a-kind, fun-loving babe will race around the house with a blankie-cape making a superhero out of your precious darling. With seemingly more changes than the accompanying number of diapers in those beginning years, your little one's growing capabilities and confidence provide endless hours of home entertainment for your family. Keep your camera close at hand and the memories even closer by creating authentic keepsake pages to celebrate each talent, trait, trick and quirk that makes your baby uniquely yours.

Griffin, giving you a bath is quite the adventure, an exercise in persuasion. You are excited to get in, you try to leave before you are washed and then you don't want to get out when it's time. Luckily, you love your froggy towel, and with it, I can wheedle you out. You run around in it, take it off, want me to put it back on and make the cutest ribbit noises; and when it's time to get dressed, you get mad. By the end, I'm exhausted, but at least you're clean (for about two minutes anyway).

froggy

(rIbbiT RIbbIt)

APR 20 2007

Playful bath towels can provide for innovative takes on bath-time pages, as Kara proves here with this amphibian-themed delight. Integrate a dynamic die-cut into your title, as shown here, to provide an eye-pleasing flow across your entire layout. Try playing around with new uses for common accessories for a thematic effect. Kara created the look of frog eyes peeking around her photo using two mini clips.

FROGGY *by Kara Henry*

Supplies: Cardstock; patterned paper (Paper Salon); letter stickers (American Crafts, EK Success); rub-ons (Scrapworks); clips (Making Memories); rickrack (Wrights); die-cut shape (Craft ROBO); Misc: pen, thread

Car rides, baby swings and now even cat beds—whatever it takes to get our little ones to nap! Shannon designed this adorable display of unusual naptime bliss around the colors and stripes of her photo. For a unique way to frame tiny photos, try cutting small pictures into tiny circles, attaching to large brads and then coating with a dimensional adhesive. Add additional embellishment by surrounding the personalized mini frames with an assortment of color coordinating mini brads.

CAT NAP *by Shannon Taylor*

Supplies: Cardstock; patterned paper (A2Z); chipboard letters (BasicGrey); brads (American Crafts, Bazzill, Junkitz); Misc: Kaylee font, glossy top coat

Oh, how our teeny chatterboxes love to babble once they discover their voices! Melanie chose soft shades, curved lines and simple stitching to create a cozy look. And flowers add a sweet touch to this adorable baby girl page. To punch up paper flowers like Melanie did, apply lines of chalk ink to emphasize the embossed petals, and add buttons or brads to add more dimension. With this simple trick you'll have a pretty layout in no time!

SHE TALKS TO THE ANIMALS *by Melanie Douthit*

Supplies: Cardstock; patterned paper (BasicGrey); chipboard letters (Heidi Swapp, Scenic Route) rub-on letters (Scenic Route); flowers (Prima); buttons (Autumn Leaves); Misc: Kabel Bk Bt font, ink

Watching your tiny tot in the process of learning a new trick is nearly as fun as the end result. Capture a series of your little learner in action to create a sequenced layout of her new trick. When using images to tell a story, as Athena did here, keep your title and background simple, and your embellishments spare to keep the focus on the event.

CLAP *by Athena Mejia*

Supplies: Cardstock; letter stickers (American Crafts); flower (My Mind's Eye); journaling card (7gypsies); Misc: acrylic paint, pen

Precious pictures!

Trying to capture every moment can be overwhelming. When snapping photos to scrapbook, focus on just a few fabulous poses.

- *Baby's silly expressions*
- *Baby crying*
- *Baby curled up asleep*
- *Baby sleeping on someone's tummy*
- *Baby clapping hands or playing a game like peek-a-boo*

- *Baby dressed in a silly hat or outfit*
- *Baby's hand holding a parent's fingers*
- *Baby with a favorite toy*
- *Baby and pet together*
- *Baby being fed*
- *Baby trying to feed self*

Some children love to ham it up before the camera; others are camera shy. Then there are some who are simply curious about the camera itself. Mandie captured her son's determination to get his hands on her camera on this freestyle collage of intentionally uneven papers. A few vertical strips to balance a vertical title are all that are needed to create whimsy but keep the eye focused on the photo.

REACH *by Mandie Pierce*

Supplies: Cardstock; patterned paper, rub-ons (KI Memories); letter stickers (American Crafts); Misc: ink, marker, thread

Knowing how to ham it up and wait for the ensuing laughter seems to be an inborn trait. Capture your little one's cheesy and charming expressions on cheerful digital designs like Amy's. Amy arranged her photos, encased in altered and overlapping digital frames, along with a fabric swatch and complementary virtual ephemera to create a look of building blocks on her page. Scalloped edges and stitched accents give any computer-generated creation traditional charm.

SAY CHEESE *by Amy Knepper*

Supplies: Image editing software (Adobe); cream background, title strip by Jessica Bolton (Scrapbook Graphics); brown background by Kristie David (Shabby Princess); graph paper by Eve Recinella (Sweet Shoppe); fabric mat, frames by Tracy Ann Robinson (Scrapbook Bytes); circle stitch, ledger paper by Anita Stergiou (Natural Designs); stitch by Lisa Whitney (ScrapArtist); letter by Misty Caro (Scrapbook Elements); cross stitches, flower by Anne Dejong (Funky Playground); heart brad by Loreta Labarca (Natural Designs); Misc: Highland Park font

Let your little charmer's image do the talking. Allow a precious portrait to shine when offset by a simple design. Heather's clean, graphic look provides enough visual interest by overlapping shapes slightly off-kilter, balancing angles in opposing directions with the contrasting roundness of a variety of circles. Plus, chipper rub-on accents give a hint of adorable whimsy to keep the look light and create a visual triangle of fun.

SWEET CHARM *by Heather Bowser*

Supplies: Cardstock; patterned paper (Scenic Route); chipboard letters (American Crafts); rub-ons (Hambly); Misc: SP Toby Unleashed font

Who could resist the twinkling eyes, cherub cheeks and dimpled grins of miniature charmers? Try a clean-line page like Jen's, which highlights the adorable face of her own little heartbreaker, using either traditional or digital supplies. Simple patterns, basic colors and limited embellishment keep the focus on charming cheeks.

CHARMER *by Jennifer Armentrout*

Supplies: Image editing software (Adobe); papers by Jessica Sprague (Creating Keepsakes); Misc: CK Classical, CK Fluid and CK Happy Circles fonts

Every baby can be a star on a magazine-inspired layout like Mindy's. A close-up of your cover model can grace one page while bold letters and journaling complete the look of a popular periodical. Choose an element, such as circles in similar patterned papers, to connect your two pages.

Supplies: Cardstock; patterned paper (BasicGrey); rub-on letters (Arctic Frog); Misc: Verdana font

CUTE EXPRESSIONS *by Mindy Bush*

Reference books you won't find at Barnes & Noble...

A guide to interpreting Katherine's vocabulary at almost One Year of Age.
(First ed., January 21, 2007)

da, *n.* 1 daddy. 2 dog.

da, *v. t.* look at that.

eee, *interj.* I'm very happy right now.

hooohh, *interj.* [pronounced on prolonged exhalation] Wow, that's just the coolest thing ever! See fig. 1.

gah, *n.* cat.

ma, *n.* mama. Also multiple repetitions, e.g. mama, mamama.

ma, *interj.* I need something. Also multiple repetitions, e.g. mama, mamama.

mmm, *adj.* yummy. See fig. 2.

ooh lala, *interj.* I like that and it makes me happy. Milder form of hooohh.

oo, oo, *n.* sound made by dog, i.e. woof, woof. Also "da oo oo."

who da, *v. t.* [breathy pronunciation, generally accompanied by pointed forefinger] 1 look. 2 tell me what that is. See fig. 3.

SNORPISMS

Experiencing childhood alongside your little one is like entering a foreign land, with even a new language to learn. As your child is desperately trying to learn to speak like you, you have to learn to play interpreter. In years to come, you will love looking back at the language the two of you shared, when captured on a creative layout of definitions. Jennifer's print-filled page gives translations of her daughter's one-year-old vocabulary, along with photos illustrating the curious expressions.

SNORPISMS *by Jennifer Mayer*

Supplies: Cardstock; patterned paper (Autumn Leaves); decorative tape (7gypsies); rub-ons (American Crafts); Misc: LDJ Mothers Typewriter font

Once your infant takes to crawling, the adventure begins for both the little one exploring and for the rest of the family trying to keep up! Sanded edges on chipboard letters add texture to any layout, but lend a rugged, outdoorsy effect to pages featuring your child's newfound mobility. Shannon found a great way to use up the negative space in her focal point photo by employing it as the backdrop for both her title and journaling. This allowed room for more images of her daughter in motion to be incorporated on the page.

ADVENTURE *by Shannon Brouwer*

Supplies: Cardstock; patterned paper (Imaginisce); chipboard letters (Daisy D's); letter stickers (American Crafts, KI Memories); button, stamp (Autumn Leaves); photo corner (KI Memories); Misc: 2Ps Quirky font, adhesive foam, ink, thread

You insisted on feeding yourself today. "Mmmmm" you would say, after each messy bite. It didn't seem to phase you that you had prunes dripping from just about every body part by the time you were finished. Prunes make an ugly mess, but they sure are good.

yummy
{ugly} prunes

As your baby grows, so will her streak of independence, and wanting to do things herself, her way. So keep that camera handy! Images like Samantha's showing her "experiential" eater make for yummy memory pages, ensuring smiles to last a lifetime. To transfer your own child's messy moments onto the page, try adding embellishments with inked edges, such as these chipboard letters inked with a sponge.

YUMMY UGLY PRUNES *by Samantha Walker*

Supplies: Cardstock; chipboard letters, patterned paper (Collage Press); rickrack (SEI); scalloped border (Doodlebug); Misc: Garamond font, brads, ink, pen

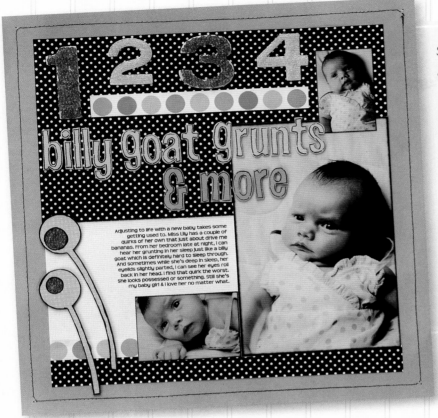

Adjusting to life with a new baby takes some getting used to. Miss Lily has a couple of quirks of her own that just about drive me bananas. From her bedroom late at night, I can hear her grunting in her sleep just like a billy goat which is definitely hard to sleep through. And sometimes while she's deep in sleep, her eyelids slightly parted, I can see her eyes roll back in her head. I find that quirk the worst. She looks possessed or something. Still she's my baby girl & I love her no matter what.

Some of our children's quirks are hands-down adorable, while others can be quite maddening. Shannon created this festive and fancy design to commemorate the comedic side of this little one's bedtime grunts and freaky expressions. Capture the same dazzle on your own layout by covering chipboard letters and accents with dimensional adhesive, and then sprinkling with miniature glass beads.

BILLY GOAT GRUNTS *by Shannon Taylor*

Supplies: Cardstock; patterned paper (A2Z); chipboard letters (American Crafts); chipboard flower and number (Fancy Pants); Misc: brads, glossy topcoat, paint, pen

Never before were boogies and dribble so adorable than when offset by your infant's big blue peepers and that little smile that turns your heart into its own pile of goo! When creating thematic pages that feature your babe's ooey, gooey quirks, think outside the box. Lana turned flourishes on edge, set alongside squiggly patterned paper to reflect the nonstop flow of baby's drips and drool.

BOOGIE & SPIT
by Lana Rappette

Supplies: Cardstock; patterned paper (Creative Imaginations, Sweetwater); letter stickers (Heidi Swapp); die-cut accents (Bam Pop); letter stickers (Chatterbox); rub-ons; Misc: King Cool font, pen, sticker accents

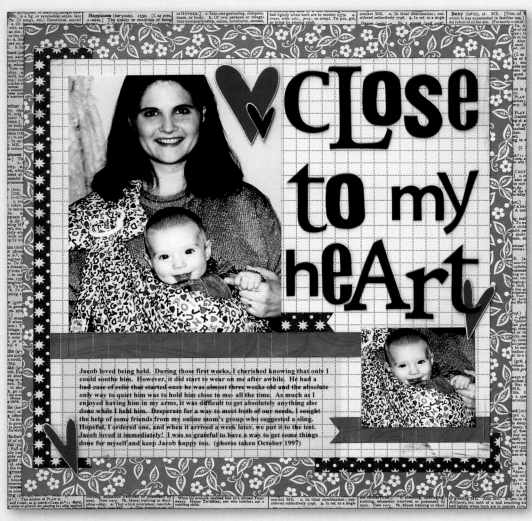

Colleen showcases her gratitude toward a comfy sling in this cozy layout. A decorative pattern pulled from your photos is a great source of inspiration for choosing your color scheme. As Colleen demonstrates, an eye-catching look can be formed by emphasizing one color found in an ornate object in the photos, pulling it throughout your page and incorporating patterns of a similar size.

CLOSE TO MY HEART *by Colleen Stearns*

Supplies: Patterned paper (7gypsies, Autumn Leaves, Jenni Bowlin, Scenic Route); chipboard letters and hearts (Heidi Swapp); Misc: ink, staples, transparency

On the "write" track!

When you're out of words to write, try one of these prompts to get your journaling juices flowing.

- *The meaning of your child's name or the story behind it*
- *Ways your daily life has changed since baby's arrival*
- *Your baby's daily routine*
- *Things your infant has taught you already*
- *Your expectations for baby's first year*

- *Hilarious habits and quirky personality traits of baby*
- *Baby's favorites*
- *Life in your household described from baby's perspective*
- *Things you love best about having a baby in the house*
- *Top 10 things you love about the little one*

No doubt about it, you're a girly girl! I'm not quite sure how that happened since I was quite the tomboy myself as a child. I suppose I could blame all of it on the pink dresses and sleepers that were gifted to us but the truth is, WE were the ones who bought you those adorable pink princess Robeez shoes. And WE are the ones who, every day, still prefer to dress you in cute frilly summery dresses. All fashion aside, the core of you is also very girly. It is easy to see in the way you move and the way you behave. These pictures capture your inner girly-ness perfectly. I just love you my girl, and I can't wait to see if you will be a tomboy too, once you can choose your clothes and activities yourself!

Even without her frilly dresses and all-pink accessories, Ann's little princess is a girl through and through. Design a pretty-in-pink layout like this one to capture the heart of your own girly girl. Rose patterned paper for a background sets the tone of the page, while a pretty turquoise block provides contrast for photos, journaling and title. Finish by accentuating floral accents with bling, such as these shimmering embellishments adorned with gems.

YOU'RE SO GIRLY *by Ann Costen*

Supplies: Cardstock; patterned paper (Chatterbox); chipboard letters, plastic flowers (American Crafts); rhinestones (Doodlebug); Misc: Courier New font, brads, silver stickers

A sewing machine is a great addition to your store of scrapbook tools. Stitches add warmth, charm and cozy comfort to a baby-themed page. Baby pages also benefit from the texture and dimension that stitches provide, and the look coordinates well with embellishments like buttons and bows. Try adding stitches as a photo or page frame, or go all out like Ruth did, with messy lines and whimsical butterfly flights.

EMMA, THAT THING YOU DO
by Ruth Akers

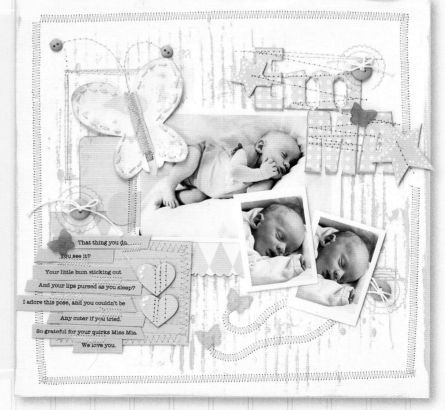

That thing you do......
You see it?
Your little bum sticking out
And your lips pursed as you sleep?
I adore this pose, and you couldn't be
Any cuter if you tried.
So grateful for your quirks Miss Mia.
We love you.

Supplies: Cardstock; chipboard letters, patterned paper, stamps (Paper Salon); buttons, chipboard hearts and stars (American Crafts); butterflies (Jesse James); Misc: elastic, paint, thread

Let your layout roll with the flow of the ocean on beach baby themed page designs, filled with rickrack, scalloped edges and polka-dot patterns. All things curvy, wavy and round evoke a sense of motion like rolling waves washing over your design in visual delight. Half circles serve double duty as homes for both title and journaling, and when balanced, as Samantha shows here, can add a rolling wave effect to pull the eye across the entire page.

WATER BABY *by Samantha Walker*

Supplies: Cardstock; chipboard, die-cut strips, patterned paper (Creative Imaginations); metal charms (SEI); decorative strips (Doodlebug); die-cut letters (Sizzix); Misc: adhesive foam, brads, decorative scissors, pen

Anything and everything is fair game to a little one's curiosity, as they set out exploring their world. With camera in tow you can often catch them jumping right in to experience the world—feet first! A large zigzag stitched border around Staci's main portion of the layout guides the eye to the center of her page. For an easy way to mix it up a bit, follow Staci's example by flowing your title into your journaling space.

CURIOUS *by Staci Compher*

Supplies: Patterned paper (BasicGrey, Scenic Route); letter stickers (Rusty Pickle); number stickers (Making Memories); journaling accent (Heidi Swapp); rub-ons (Creative Imaginations); plastic brackets (Queen & Co.); Misc: pen

Babies' favorite pastimes are limited at this age, but bath time ranks high on the list for many! Mou found a home for this sweet black-and-white image of her son's bath-time ritual, here on this tub-time classic. To re-create this look on your own pages, trim patterned paper slightly smaller than your printed transparency and staple it behind. Try Mou's trick for transparencies: Brush a wash of color over the transparency to create a colorful space for journaling, then use the same paint color to create a photo frame.

BATH *by Mou Saha*

Supplies: Patterned paper (Die Cuts With A View); transparency (Creative Imaginations); transparent letters (Heidi Swapp); brackets (Bo-Bunny); sticker accents (7gypsies, Pebbles); Misc: acrylic paint, pen, ruler, staples

Got photos that don't match anything in your scrapbooking collection? Photo editing to the rescue! Lana neutralized the busy striped shirt in her photos by switching them to black and white. To create a cohesive design, Lana used patterns in similar hues and added strips of the same paper under each of her supporting photos. Lana played up her page's theme by arranging arrows and title letters in an upward motion, adding visual interest and playfulness to the design.

TOES UP *by Lana Rappette*

Supplies: Patterned paper (Creative Imaginations, Making Memories, Prima); letter stickers (Making Memories); rub-on letters (American Crafts); word stickers (Heidi Grace); swirl accent (Creative Imaginations); tag (SEI); arrow brad (Around the Block); chipboard arrow (KI Memories); Misc: pen

ELI

Don't touch MY PACIFIER

Pacifier. Binky. Woppy. Fier. Paci. Plug. Savior. Friend... Whatever you call it, this sweet little invention is a God-send. Eli is rarely seen without this contraption plugging up his mouth. The only downfall to having a baby hooked is that at least once a week, it is inevitable that of the 15 pacifiers floating around the house, you will be able to locate exactly zero. They will eventually turn up in the toy box, the dishwasher, the corner of the bedroom, the car seat, your pants' pocket, and just about everywhere else you can imagine. I guess it's just one of the joys of having a baby!

So Happy Together

The love affair between a child and his pacifier is a match made in heaven, as Courtney's tribute piece attests. Courtney based her entire design around the colors and stripes found in this photo of her nephew. Stripes in the patterned paper echo the stripes in the shirt creating a cohesive design. Courtney also employed a visual triangle in her design by placing the three phrases in separate points around the page.

MY PACIFIER *by Courtney Walsh*

Supplies: Cardstock; patterned paper, ribbon (Chatterbox); rub-on letters (KI Memories); chipboard letters (Making Memories); popsicle stick (BasicGrey); Misc: Century Gothic font, pen

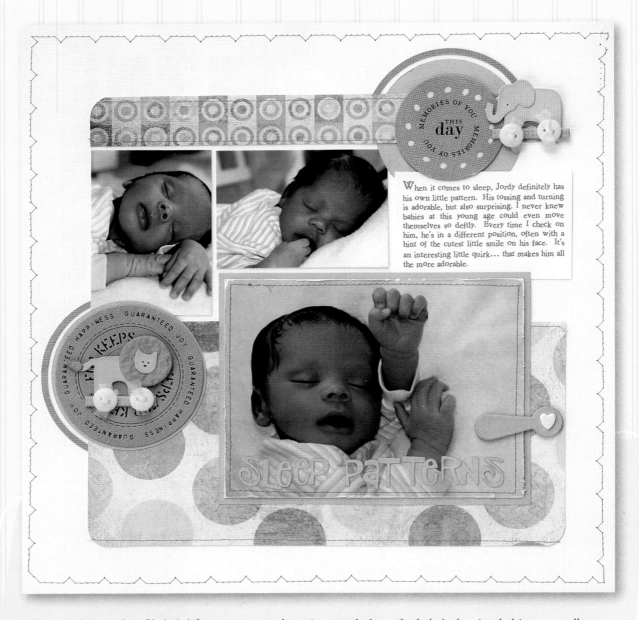

When it comes to sleep, Jordy definitely has his own little pattern. His tossing and turning is adorable, but also surprising. I never knew babies at this young age could even move themselves so deftly. Every time I check on him, he's in a different position, often with a hint of the cutest little smile on his face. It's an interesting little quirk... that makes him all the more adorable.

Those early months of baby's life equate to random times and places for baby's sleeping habits…as well as mom's! Cherish the images of your little angel at rest on sweet, dreamy designs like Lisa's. Lisa played up the polka dots in her patterned papers by adding animal shape embellishments with button accents and adding in free-wheeling fun created by a circle cutter. The white, stitched border adds to the theme by creating a cloud-like effect.

SLEEP PATTERNS *by Lisa Tutman-Oglesby*

Supplies: Cardstock; patterned paper (BasicGrey); die-cut letters (QuicKutz); rub-ons (Creative Imaginations); heart brad (Making Memories); animal shapes (Westrim); Misc: acrylic paint, circle cutter, pen, thread

Supplies: Cardstock; patterned paper (Daisy Bucket); rub-on letters (American Crafts, Dollarama); rub-on accents (Hambly); journaling tab (Heidi Swapp); Misc: hole punch, ink, pen

Whether your snuggle bug loves to snooze or thinks life's too short for napping, her sleep habits are a hot topic in any circle of empathetic moms. Claude created this dreamy display of dots and doodles around the humorous nickname of her no-napping sweetheart. To create the look of layered squares, Claude first cut out a square from her orange cardstock, inked the edges and then glued it back in place. You can create your own dot pattern like Claude's with an eyelet punch to reveal the color of the paper beneath.

KIRA-NO-NAP *by Claude Campeau*

Babies do their best to fight the good fight in keeping their little eyes open, but eventually eyes get heavy and the sandman always wins. Send images of your own sleep warrior off to dreamland on a comfy, cozy layout like Samantha's. The title for this page really says it all, with "e's" turned upside down like half-shut eyes, and the second word slowly drifting down the page to the photo. Overlapped semicircles lend a lunar effect, while a decorative ribbon tucks babe snugly onto this rich and dreamy design.

SLEEPY GIRL *by Samantha Walker*

Supplies: Patterned paper (BasicGrey, Creative Imaginations); adhesive fabric (Making Memories); chipboard letters, plastic flowers (Heidi Swapp); paper flowers (Prima); Misc: Garamond font, brads, ink

sleepy girl

You fight it...your eyes get heavy, and so you rub them. You will do everything in your power to stay awake, but face it, Sydney, you're a sleepy girl. I watch your eyelids sink lower and lower, then you open them again with a little squawk and a scream. You cry because you don't want to miss a thing. But little, Sydney, there isn't anything you can do to fix it, you have to give in to sleep.

THE INTENSE STARE

We get this alot, such a serious little guy.

Sometimes our babies are happy as can be and other times they're in a fit of tears. And then there are those moments when they seem so serious, as if they are looking right through us in wonder. Mindy transferred the essence of her little guy's serious side by including a simple but large photo that really makes an impact. Subtle patterns, a simple block title and a triad of star shapes complete the look while drawing attention to the journaling strip.

INTENSE STARE *by Mindy Bush*   Supplies: *Misc: patterned paper, ribbon, chipboard stars*

Sometimes a baby's hair just can't decide what to do! Sheila took a humorous approach in designing this spread, featuring the bare patch on the back of her son's head. Play up this theme for your own child, using spotted paper and mini brads to reiterate the title.

BALD SPOT *by Sheila Doherty*

"This is not a *bald* spot... it's a solar panel for brain power." · Unknown

All of my kids have gotten bald spots on the back of their heads as infants. But Ty's, his was the most evident. It seemed as if his hair just stopped growing all together in that spot and the hair above it had been trimmed in a straight line. And it was that way for months! He was over a year old before his hair got the message to start growing again and that spot filled in. Just one of those marks of infancy I guess. Looking on the bright side, maybe having a bald spot now will prevent him from having them later in life?

Tyler · 7 months

Supplies: Cardstock; patterned paper (Scrapworks); Misc: BlackJack and Century fonts, brads

Whether your child has a headful of curls, an adorable little cowlick, or a wild and crazy mess of tresses, pages like Lisa's are fun ways to cherish baby's first 'do. Shapes and elements that capture the look of your child's hair personality make for an expressive page design, as Lisa demonstrates by utilizing star patterns to play up the wide and spiky angles of her son's hair. A circular border around her "mane" photo and a sequin-mask background soften the sharp lines with balancing contrast.

HAIR *by Lisa Hoel*

Supplies: Patterned paper (Scenic Route); letter stamps (Michaels); chipboard arrow (Deluxe Designs); rub-ons (Melissa Frances); clip, snaps (Making Memories); die-cut file folder (Sizzix); Misc: adhesive foam, ink, pen

heaven sent

DATE 3/07   TOPIC Auntie Jodi's
email to family
and friends...

"When I saw her for the first time, it was like I knew she was coming all along. A connection that I cannot explain. Maybe it's because she's a female, and all of us females stick together! Or was it because I just knew that "she" would come. I felt it in my heart. Tears came to my eyes when I held her, she was so sweet and awake! Her eyes bright eyed and ready for the world! She is the most beautiful thing I've ever seen. Like a breathe of fresh air in front of a blue sea. She left me speechless!! "

special memories

chapter

FOUR

a family affair

Few things in life have the same transformative power as the arrival
of a baby into a family. As that first cry of life breaks through the air,
seemingly ordinary adults, in an instant, become someone's world.
Parents become grandparents. Other children take on titles of big
bro or sis. And the list goes on, as aunts, uncles, cousins and more
all respond with outstretched arms. How blessed is the baby who has
so many people to love and be loved by; and to have as cheerleaders
as little one takes those first step and who will keep on cheering with
each proceeding step in life to follow. Memory pages that celebrate a
child's bond with relatives reaffirm how deeply and plentifully he or
she is loved. Such layouts not only illustrate how a child is part
of a family, they express how a child is part of a family's
legacy—a legacy that will continue to transform lives for
many more generations and memory albums to come.

Incorporating visual triangles on baby pages is a great and simple way to achieve an eye-pleasing design. A visual triangle can be created from any page element: colors, embellishments, words, photos. Here, Heather positioned three silk flowers in a triangle on her layout, which draws the eye to the artfully unfocused focal point photo. She created a secondary visual triangle with three half-circles, which leads the eye to follow the simple story around the page.

B & L *by Heather Bowser*

Supplies: Cardstock; patterned paper (BasicGrey); letter stickers (KI Memories); ampersand sticker (American Crafts); flowers (Bazzill); Misc: Blissful font, brads

Hugs one minute. Bites the next. Such is the life of brothers. Eric and Benjamin. February 2007.

Heartfelt humor abounds on this behind-the-scenes layout, featuring a focal point image filled with brotherly love and candid close-ups. Capture this look on your own sibling salutes by positioning a loving image of your children with accent photos revealing the other side of affection. A look like Jennifer's can be created traditionally or via digital means.

LOVE *by Jennifer Armentrout*

Supplies: Image editing software (Adobe); paper and accents (Digital Scrapbook Memories); hearts (Two Peas in a Bucket); chipboard hearts (artist's own design); Misc: AL Modern Type and Arial fonts, floss, tissue paper

2 little boys. brothers! You already adore each other but I can't wait to see what the future holds! Stay close!

Vicky illustrates the sibling bond on this cuddly creation dedicated to the way her son eagerly embraces his newborn brother. Vicky kept her layout simple to keep focus on the photo. Serene green and blue colors lend a natural look to the page, while swift white brushstrokes give a boyish, rough-around-the-edges grit. Vicky added rub-ons and letter stickers to the paint to accentuate the title block.

THEN THERE WERE *2 by Vicky Gibson*

Supplies: Cardstock; number sticker, patterned paper (American Crafts); letter stickers (Heidi Swapp, Scenic Route) rub-ons (Heidi Swapp); Misc: paint, pen

On the scrapbook layout:
brother & sister
happy memory
beginnings

hello

July 17 —
one day old. Thomas met his
new sister. He was fascinated
by her feet & toes and
kept unwrapping the
blanket to look at them.

Ribbons and bows, stitching and buttons: they all provide a soft and cozy, comfy and warm feel for baby layouts. But they're not your only option. Whether you're out of embellishments or simply looking for something simple, look no further than the most basic supply. Try tearing patterned paper to create soft and simple edges, just the right bit of texture for tender themes like Deborah's. Think about ways you take your supplies beyond the basics for fresh and easy new designs.

HELLO *by Deborah Mahnken*

Supplies: Patterned paper (7gypsies, BasicGrey, Imagination Project); letter stickers (American Crafts); word stickers (EK Success); chipboard (Deluxe Designs); button, die-cut tag (My Mind's Eye); Misc: pen

All in the family!

Check out these topic ideas for creating family keepsake pages.

- *Comparison of baby's and another family member's physical traits*
- *Special bonds with relatives*
- *Sibling relations and rivalries*
- *Baby's bond with family pets*

- *Relatives feeding baby a bottle*
- *Introduction of baby to relatives*
- *Photos of family's hands or feet together*
- *Loved one's advice or well-wishes for baby*
- *The new number of people in your family*

Even if your letters are the same, it doesn't mean your title has to be plain. Sherry added a wash of pastel color to jazz up the title for this vintage and feminine layout. But she didn't stop there. She added a large pearly button to stand in for the letter "o" and turned the "h" on its side to give the classic layout a twist. On your next layout, try to think about how can you can mix things up just a bit with a spin on a single embellishment.

BROTHER *by Sherry Wright*

Supplies: Cardstock; chipboard letters and frame, die-cut shapes, patterned paper, rub-ons, stamp (Paper Salon); Misc: buttons, ink, lace, transparency

Printing words on a transparency or vellum is the perfect way to easily print a piece of text without distracting from the look of the layout. Using these materials allows you to create journaling on a separate sheet from background cardstock, but still allows colors and patterns to shine through. And on Jennifer's layout, vellum completes the look well, echoing the sheerness of the ribbons.

THIS IS LOVE *by Jennifer Richards*

Supplies: Cardstock; chipboard letters, letter stickers over chipboard, patterned paper, ribbon (All My Memories); die-cut letters (QuicKutz); buttons (EK Success); Misc: Susie's Hand font, staples, vellum

He said "I am whAt I Am" He tipped

named SaM.

here once was a monkey

is hand & twitched his

ta i Ě SA i d l Am of te AL3Ba m"

SAM I AM

Sadie—
Even though it would
be years before you
could really read to
your little sister, you
still tried your hardest
to relay this little rhyme
that Mamaw made up
when I was little. It
is no wonder that
Madison adores you!
xoxo
Nana

August 2001

A love for literacy is a precious bond between family members and a trait to be passed down for generations. Sandi captured her daughters' connection over a family rhyme on this whimsical party on paper. Wanting to use a cheery strip of argyle patterned paper, but finding the original hues too bright for her layout, Sandi solved the problem by spraying a white wash spray over top in several layers to achieve a perfect match.

SAM I AM *by Sandi Minchuk*

Supplies: Cardstock; chipboard animal, patterned paper, scalloped cardstock (Die Cuts With A View); chipboard letters (Pressed Petals); letter stickers (American Crafts, Making Memories); white wash spray (Krylon); Misc: ink, paint, pen, thread

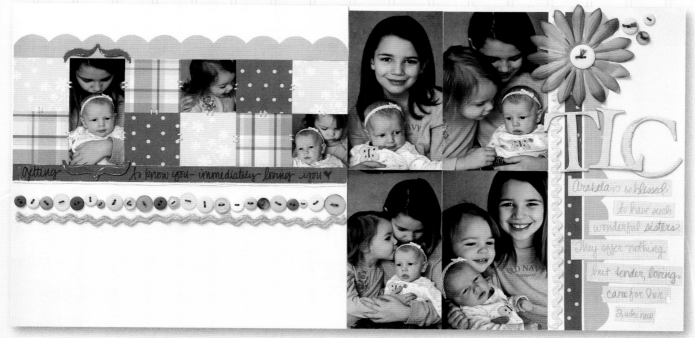

Maegan wanted to evoke a sense of welcoming love on her layout. To create a warm and comfy layout like Maegan's, try a two-page spread filled with buttons, rickrack and sanded edges for softness, and incorporate the look of a quilt across an entire page. Simply cut a variety of patterned paper scraps into 2" x 2" (5cm x 5cm) blocks and stitch together.

TLC *by Maegan Hall*

Supplies: Cardstock; patterned paper (Chatterbox); chipboard letters (Heidi Swapp); buttons (Autumn Leaves, Doodlebug, Making Memories); rickrack (Doodlebug, unknown); Misc: acrylic paint, floss, flower

The indelible bond between sisters is not possible to describe fully with words, but pages such as Kathie's do well to visually express the emotion of this special love. Rich and intricate elements, such as fanciful scrolls covered in jewel-toned cardstock and glittery hearts, lend a sense of royalty and elegance to the design. Try flowing your own title around your page for movement and an effect that complements the look of the scrolls.

A SISTER'S LOVE *by Kathie Davis*

Supplies: Cardstock; buttons, chipboard accents, patterned paper (Rusty Pickle); chipboard letters (Heidi Swapp); bird and hearts (hand cut by artist); Misc: glitter, pen

The connection between little ones as they bond together as family and friends is a beautiful experience. Terri captured the innocence of such untainted love through light airy colors and dreamy, free-spirited digital patterns and stamps downloaded into this visual delight. When layering similar images like these, it helps to add an element, such as the digital ribbon or photo border, to distinguish the pictures and pull the eye to the focal-point shot.

INTRO *by Terri Davenport*

Supplies: Image editing software (Adobe); page kit, stamps and stitching brushes by Katie Pertiet (Designer Digitals); Misc: Charlesworth and Hopscotch Plain fonts

Since he is baby #3, I act quickly on anything I do. One time saver is big sister Lucy acting as his resident Guardian. When I need to step away to wash my hands; she's there. If I run for a new package of wipes; she's there. Got a phone call? She's there. He dropped his bottle? She's there. She's always there.

If you're stuck with a mishmash of random letters, don't throw them out! Follow Lana's lead and paint them the same color. Even letters of different sizes and weights will look unified on your page. To make your title shine without lots of bling, apply a small bit of shimmer paint or dimensional adhesive to the letters. For a final punch, tie on a glossy button to use at the dot for an "i" or "j."

GUARDIAN *by Lana Rappette*

Supplies: Cardstock; patterned paper (Creative Imaginations); chipboard letters (Imagination Project, Li'l Davis, Making Memories); ribbon (May Arts); tag (SEI); sticker (Heidi Grace); buttons, rub-ons (Autumn Leaves); swirl accents (Designfruit); Misc: Tekton Pro font, floss, paint

Inspiration for a layout can happen in an instant, as it was with Trina's touching tribute to her twins. Seeing their little legs and feet intertwined served as a reminder of how twins' lives are linked from conception. Painted flourishes accompanied by a glittery glow provide embellishment that echoes the page's intertwining theme.

MEMORIES FOREVER *by Trina McClune*

legs entwined as your life will be always siblings twins family through the good and bad

Supplies: Patterned paper (Daisy D's, Fancy Pants); chipboard words (Li'l Davis); clock and heart accents (Heidi Swapp); ribbon (7gypsies); stamps (Hero Arts); Misc: acrylic paint, floss, flowers, glitter, ink, staples, tags

"i'll do it!"

Volunteerism must come naturally to Oliver because he offered to babysit his new cousin Anna just hours after she was born. Instead, we just let him hold her. He was pleased!

Older children can't resist the magnetic draw of a new baby in the family, and want to help in any way they can. Capture the enthusiasm with a splash of color on your page. By simply painting your background in a hue matching your photo's background, you will achieve a unified look. Plus, rugged brushstrokes lend a boyish streak to the design.

I'LL DO IT! *by Shannon Taylor*

Supplies: Cardstock; patterned paper (A2Z); chipboard letters (American Crafts); tag (Making Memories); hearts (Heidi Grace); Misc: Whackadoo font, floss, paint

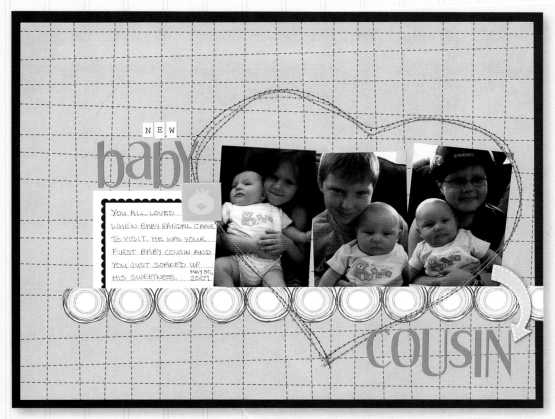

Supplies: Cardstock; patterned paper (Creative Imaginations); letter stickers (Arctic Frog, EK Success); chipboard accents (American Crafts, Doodlebug); Misc: pen, thread

Kissin' cousins take center stage on heartwarming layouts like Annette's. To achieve this same look of family bonding on your own page designs, group individual photos of your babe with his loved ones together, and then stitch a heart around the overall arrangement using a variety of threads. Annette chose a clean patterned paper with lines that create the illusion of stitches, and added cut patterned paper circles for a homespun effect.

NEW BABY COUSIN
by Annette Pixley

Older children make for big helpers, especially when it comes to bottle-feeding baby. Be sure to capture many images of the special bond that magically occurs between a child and your little one over a shared meal. Colleen embraced her touching photos on this sweet design, inspired by the flowers on baby's pj's. For further feminine fun, accentuate the frill of pink translucent flowers with a variety of girly brads.

I SO LOVE THIS *by Colleen Stearns*

Supplies: Cardstock, patterned paper (Creative Imaginations, Heidi Grace); letter stickers (SEI); chipboard (Heidi Grace); flowers (Heidi Swapp); ribbon (May Arts); tag (Staples); Misc: brads, ink, lace, pen

FinaLLY!

I have A nephew

As an aunt to five nieces, I was thrilled to know that my baby sister Lori was expecting my first nephew! I adore little Jimmy so much! (7/05)

The thrill of a new niece or nephew expresses itself in heartfelt pages, like Colleen's all-boy tribute to her newborn nephew. A complementary color scheme of pale blue and green creates a masculine environment for heartwarming photos, while maintaining a baby soft style. Scalloped edges and hints of ribbon enhance the innocent look of this page capturing the joy that blossoms as a loving family grows.

FINALLY *by Colleen Stearns*

Supplies: Patterned paper (Chatterbox, Crate Paper, Creative Imaginations, Heidi Grace); letter stickers (Making Memories); ribbon (May Arts); arrow and word stickers (EK Success); Misc: ink, pen

Get out of the (journaling) box! Whether you're looking for something different for each baby page, or have simply run out of words, you can tap different sources for journaling thoughts. Try finding quotes or poems that express the right sentiment, look in recent journal entries or turn to correspondence. Authentic journaling from an e-mail Robyn's sister sent served as the inspiration behind this cheery layout and is the perfect personal touch for her journaling.

HEAVEN SENT *by Robyn Lantz*

Supplies: Cardstock; patterned paper (Creative Imaginations, Heidi Grace); title stickers (Making Memories); chipboard accents (Heidi Grace); flower (Heidi Swapp); rub-ons (BasicGrey, My Mind's Eye); tag (Pebbles); rickrack (Prima); Misc: notebook paper, ribbon, staples

For a mother of all boys, news of a baby girl means finally buying all things pink, ruffly and ribboned! Shannon expressed her shopping enthusiasm toward becoming an aunt to a girl on this sugar and spice layout, sampling just a handful of the girly-girl infant outfits she couldn't resist. You can add this same dimensional arrangement to any of your designs by adhering same-size photos to thin chipboard squares and scratching the edges to create photo "frames."

AN AUNT'S ANTICIPATION
by Shannon Taylor

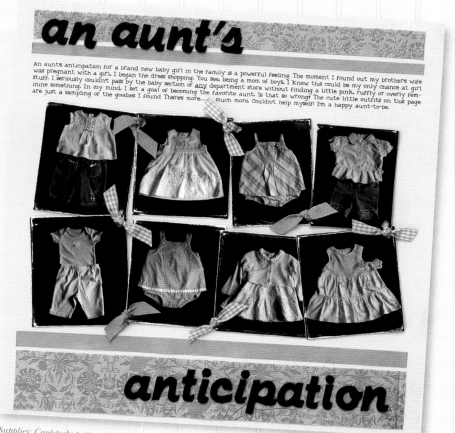

Supplies: Cardstock; patterned paper (Autumn Leaves); chipboard letters, ribbon (American Crafts); Misc: Betsystype font, paint

This picture was taken when my grandfather held his second grandchild for the very first time. He loved both his grandchildren so much. He is no longer with us now and I miss him a lot and so do the children. I do not have a lot of pictures of him so I treasure this one with all my heart.

remember

special

first

There are many firsts in a baby's first year, but a premier meeting of a great-grandparent is monumental and needs a memory page to savor the moment. Using a brown-based color scheme, like Corinne's, provides a vintage look to a layout, while accents, such as these circles done in crayon, balance an antique air with childlike charm. Add in a page torn from an old book and roughed-up edges to finish the vintage but casual effect.

SPECIAL FIRST *by Corinne Delis*

Supplies: Cardstock; chipboard heart, patterned paper (CherryArte); word stickers (Making Memories); flowers, rhinestone (Prima); arrow accent (Heidi Swapp); Misc: Typewriter font, crayons, page from old book, staples

Always the twinkle in a grandparent's eye, your child needs a special page to cherish such a beautiful bond. Lana chose her photos with one image focusing on her grandma's smiling face, and the other on her son's silly expression, aligning them so the focal point—the two expressions—remained in the center of the page. Special pages like these, with large photos and simple backgrounds, are a perfect place to use a number of favorite embellishments, grouping them together like a collage.

CHERUB *by Lana Rappette*

Supplies: Cardstock; patterned paper (Autumn Leaves); tag (SEI); flowers (Prima); stickers (Making Memories); arrow brad (Around the Block); ribbon (May Arts); cherub image (ScrapArtist); swirl accents (Designfruit); Misc: brads, decorative scissors, felt, ink, safety pin

Quality time with Grandma makes for precious pages honoring a priceless bond. Mou gave this layout a vintage effect, choosing a retro-style patterned paper which coordinated perfectly with her mother's dress. Try her unique approach of using rub-ons as photo corners. And to keep page elements from taking too much space, try Mou's trick: Tuck a tag with journaling behind the photo. The idea is both space-saving and creative!

SMITTEN *by Mou Saha*

Supplies: Cardstock; letter stickers, patterned paper (Rusty Pickle); rub-ons (7gypsies); ribbon (Offray); paper trim (Wrights); Misc: floss, hole punch, pen, tab punch

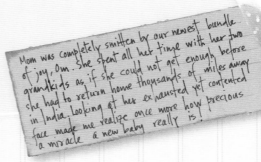

Mom was completely smitten by our newest bundle of joy, Om. She spent all her time with her two grandkids as if she could not get enough before she had to return home thousands of miles away in India. Looking at her exhausted yet contented face made me realize once more how precious a miracle a new baby really is!

for a grandmother, this is a slice of

heaven

Grammy thought that at 8 months, baby Ford had gotten too old to fall asleep in her arms. After a long day at the beach, he proved her blessedly wrong. What a precious surprise.

BABY

sweet

For baby, a day at the beach and Grandma's lap are all that are needed for a heavenly nap, as Cyndi's serene layout attests. To achieve the same dreamy look of a little one asleep, play around with digital brushes printed onto a transparency to create your own photo overlay. Minimal embellishments and transparent letters keep this look quiet, while allowing us to clearly see the accents.

SLICE OF HEAVEN
by Cyndi Michener

Supplies: Patterned paper (Autumn Leaves); scalloped paper (Karen Russell); letters (Heidi Swapp); journaling accent (Rhonna Designs); chipboard flourish (Maya Road); charms, ribbon, sticker (Making Memories); rub-ons (American Crafts); Misc: acrylic paint, pen

Grandmas are great for many reasons, but especially for sneaking candy to our babies! Jennifer captured the humor of her child and mother bonding over lollipops on this yummy, sweet page design. For your own pages showcasing love affairs with food, try choosing your colors and textures to reflect the favorite treat. Jennifer matched the vibrant color of the candy for her background and contrasted the sticky, smooth look of the lollipop with the soft texture of felt ribbon and embellishments.

REASON 438.5 *by Jennifer Mayer*

REASON 438.5

So, grandmas are more fun than moms for lots of reasons... one of them being that Grandmas give you candy while Moms think Goldfish crackers are a treat! 1-3-07

Supplies: Cardstock; patterned paper (Scenic Route); acrylic letters (KI Memories); rickrack (May Arts); felt ribbon (Queen & Co.); felt accent (Tinkering Ink); journaling accent (Creative Imaginations); Misc: paperclip, pen

FASCINATED

Pure fascination for sure! Just look at the cute face you made when you saw this little parrot! Judging by the look it gave you, I am not so sure who was more intrigued... You would look at each other and study the other's every move. If that is not fascination, I don't know what is!

Fine feathered friends of your family present themselves as quite the source of fascination for little ones. Capture the same light, spirited look on your layouts by first grounding the page with a photo enlarged to fit the width of your page. Balance out the photo with a bold, bright title and tie the look together—literally— with big buttons. And don't forget the journaling, which runs along the top of the photo.

FASCINATED
by Paola López-Araiza Osante

Supplies: Scalloped cardstock (Bazzill); patterned paper (BasicGrey, Cosmo Cricket); die-cut title (Craft ROBO); chipboard bird (Magistical Memories); buttons (Autumn Leaves); stamp (7gypsies); Misc: Ravenna font, floss, thread

Family comes in all shapes and sizes, and often with four legs and fur! Treasure the precious relationships your baby has with your pets on tender keepsake pages, like Melanie's. Machine stitching around the inner mat blends with the classic look of buttons and lace. A coordinating metal embellishment, such as this decorative leaf, gives dimensional shine and lends interest to bare space around the journaling block.

FRIENDS
by Melanie Douthit

BeSt FRIenD

There is a saying that a dog is man's best friend. Well, in our house, a puppy is a girl's best friend. You were six months old when Jasmine joined our family. She was fearless and you both became instant friends. You shared toys, the tub, & moms lap. As you got older, Jasmine liked to take naps with you. You even sometimes call her your sister, & I call you "my two girls!"

photo: August 2005
journaling: August 2007

Supplies: Cardstock; patterned paper (Dream Street); letter stickers (American Crafts); leaf accent (Nunn Design); photo corner (One Heart); buttons (Autumn Leaves); Misc: ink, lace, pen

Buddies

When you were first born Oliver, Monkey was barely bigger than you were! He's been your constant companion, your playmate, your BUDDY!

New moms are always running out of time. But don't despair! A quick and simple page is at your finger-tips. Keepsake pages like Sheila's can be kept simple but still provide a sense of warmth as Sheila proves. She borrowed from the monkey theme, utilizing a jungle-like paper background, a mat designed from cardstock, and a single chipboard accent accompanied by a bit of handwritten journaling. Easy!

BUDDIES *by Sheila Penner*

Supplies: Patterned paper (Bo-Bunny, Sweetwater); chipboard accent (K&Co.); Misc: ink, pen

Out of **bounds**!

If a little one's smile is so cute it just has to be put on display, try these out-of-the album ideas for scrapbooking baby.

Shadow Box—These make great gifts for family members! To create one, frame a special layout with a shadow box. Then add tiny trinkets, dimensional accents and memorabilia. Embellish the frame with heartwarming accents.

Calendar—Celebrate the highlights of baby's first year. Create a calendar template and record baby's milestones each month on the calendar. Complete each month's look with patterned papers and embellishments. Bind together when the year is over.

Wall Art—Consider expanding your horizons beyond 12" x 12" (30cm x 30cm). Cover a large canvas square with paint or fabric. Then add photos, patterned papers, ribbons and other embellishments.

Memory Box—Transform a box into a keepsake treasure chest. Embellish your box with patterned papers, paint, stamps, rub-ons, even photos. Keep all your unscrapped photos and memorabilia inside.

sweet • beautiful • darling • fancy • princess • loveable • adorable • baby • girl

father's

LOVE 07

Katie, you are so sweet when you're curled up and sleeping like this. You're just so precious, we can still hardly believe you are here... and you belong to us. We're a family at last and that fills us with so much joy. I love this picture of Daddy checking to make sure that everything is OK, and that you're content in slumber. I know this hand will always be there for you in every way. We love you little girl.

Sweet serenity and complete security grace Lisa's layout in style. A black-and-white image posing a father's strong hand overtop baby's tiny shoulder creates a strong composition. A chipboard word tucks the color image in tenderly on the right and ties in with the look of the patterned paper and ribbons. By using complementary colors in shades of pink and green, Lisa balances out the femininity with a neutral accent, lending a masculine touch.

A FATHER'S LOVE *by Lisa Tutman-Oglesby*

Supplies: Cardstock; patterned paper (Creative Imaginations, SEI); chipboard word (Fancy Pants); die-cut letters (QuicKutz); number sticker (EK Success); ribbon (Michaels); flowers (Doodlebug); rub-ons (Deja Views); rhinestones (Heidi Swapp); Misc: acrylic paint, thread, transparency

It doesn't take much for a baby girl to have her daddy wrapped around her little fingers. Photos featuring formal attire call for papers and accessories with sophisticated style and elegant details. Even if your digital store includes only brushes, you can still make a page with digital embellishments. Follow Maureen's lead, and turn your brushes into a 3-D accent. Maureen simply added a drop shadow to her decorative heart and changed the color to a metal tone to give flat brushwork 3-D charm.

ADORE *by Maureen Spell*

Supplies: Image editing software (Adobe); patterned paper, tag, twisted lace (Jen Wilson); frame edgers, patterned paper by Katie Pertiet (Designer Digitals); heart brush by Jesse Edwards (Designer Digitals); staple by Leora Sanford (Designer Digitals); photo action (EZ Actions); Misc: Porcelain font

This was one of those nights when Nini, about 2 months old at the time, refused to settle down. I was frustrated and ready to give up. That's when Ashis stepped in.

When nothing worked, he flopped down on the sofa, exhausted... A few minutes later, I heard the silence... Nini was not fussy any more. She was peacefully settled in daddy's bare chest and Ashis had dozed off too!

dAddy's girl

There are always those nights where nothing seems to soothe your baby's fussiness. But in Mou's case, the soft sense of security found in Daddy's arms did the trick. A chain of daisies and pink paper give a delicate touch of femininity to the daddy-daughter design. When you have candid images, such as this one, with distracting background elements, follow this page example by concealing the background clutter with page embellishments such as hand-cut hearts.

DADDY'S GIRL *by Mou Saha*

Supplies: Patterned paper (Frances Meyer); letter stickers (American Crafts, Making Memories); stickers (7gypsies); paper trim (Wrights); ribbon (Michaels); Misc: pen, ruler, staples, thread

Like father, like son is the theme of Amy's comparison creation, highlighting the similarities between her baby and his dad. List the traits shared between your child and family members in your own designs, adding interest by emphasizing key words using various fonts or embellishments. For pages craving a more masculine approach, incorporate screw-head brads into decorative elements, like Amy's stars and title frame.

SAME *by Amy Williams*

Supplies: Cardstock; chipboard frame, letters and phrases, patterned paper (Scenic Route); stars (Heidi Swapp); brads (Eyelet Outlet); labels (Dymo)

same

amazing smile
twinkle in your eye
dashing looks
BRAVE heart
inquisitive mind
strong spirit
YOU AND DAD
2 MONTHS OLD
APRIL 2007

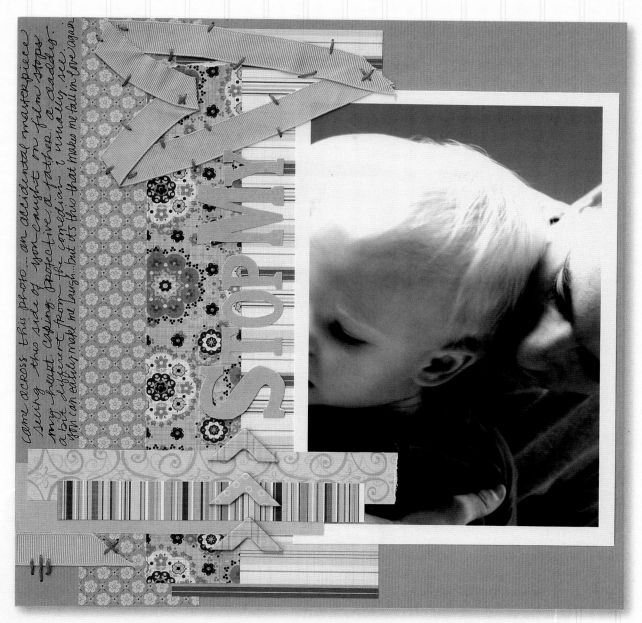

There are few things a mother finds more attractive than seeing her husband's tender side exposed in his role as daddy. Don't overlook "accidental" shots like Courtney's candid one here. Candid shots make for precious pages that celebrate fathers who love being dads. A soft blue color scheme keeps a layout looking masculine, while a hand-stitched heart created with ribbon lends a sentimental softness to precious paternal moments.

STOP MY HEART *by Courtney Walsh*

Supplies: Cardstock; patterned paper, photo corners, ribbon (Chatterbox); Misc: floss, pen

YOU ARE SO ADORED AND
LOVED. I AM ONE LUCKY MOM.

YOU AND ME
TOGETHER

Mindy's layout pays tribute to the beatifully simple relationship between mother and baby. Help your own black-and-white images pop off the page by contrasting them with patterns in cheerful tones. A single dynamic accent gives just the right amount of texture and pizzazz when set opposite sweet words. Mindy used a single journaling strip with words that suggest the soft whispers of mom into baby's ear.

YOU AND ME TOGETHER *by Mindy Bush*

Supplies: Misc: image editing software, patterned paper, die-cut flower, epoxy sticker

MUMMY & ME

My Mum didn't want to have any children. She didn't want to share Dad with anyone. Her parents didn't have a great relationship. Mum thought that every child her parents had (they had five in total) pushed them further apart. But she later realised there was more to it than that. Mum and Dad didn't realise they were pregnant with me until several months into the pregancy. "I'm so glad God had his own plans for me otherwise I wouldn't have had the joy and pleasure of four beautiful girls, each with different personalities. Thank you for your friendship and just being you."

Aug 1973

Sentimental stories of family love need cheerful pages, like Yvette's, in order to pass down the joyful insights on mother-daughter relationships that may otherwise get lost in history. Bold, beautiful colors and patterns express the unfathomable love that comes with the miracle and blessing of a baby. Stitched strips along the bottom and sanded chipboard edges add a touch of vintage chic.

MUMMY & ME
by Yvette Adams

Supplies: Cardstock; patterned paper (BasicGrey); chipboard accents (Heidi Swapp); rub-ons (Decadry, Heidi Swapp, Making Memories); Misc: thread

Two become one on Monica's tender-hearted creation. Using a flexible ruler, you can achieve a similar effect on your own designs, tracing swirls onto your layout and then writing a thematic word the entire length of them. Monica also discovered that two heads set together in a photo resemble the shape of a heart, and emphasized the look with buttons. For added dimension, stamp a word, like "love," with paint, cut it out and then set on adhesive foam squares.

A MOTHER'S LOVE
by Monica BaconRind

A mother's love

♡ love

A mother's love is an eternal flame, forever sparked by her children's own.

~Suzanne Smith

love

Supplies: Cardstock; patterned paper (BasicGrey); die-cut letters (Provo Craft); flowers (Prima); buttons (Junkitz); stamps (Autumn Leaves); heart (Heidi Swapp); flex ruler (Bo-Bunny); Misc: acrylic paint, ink, pen, staples

As I write this journal, you are already almost one year old! It's amazing how time flies. In this picture, I am 7 months pregnant with you, and I can only imagine what it will be like to be a family of six. I'm so excited about it. I've dreamed all my life of being a mother, and not only a mother, but a mother of a large family. Being a family of six is even better than I could have ever imagined. Every day is better than the day before. You and your brothers are true blessings, dreams come true, and I thank God every day for my wonderful family of six.

sis·ter [sis'tər]
n. 1. A girl or woman related to another person by having the same parents

The arrival of a baby is always a family affair; however, the larger the family, the more hearts await to share in the love. Wanting a simple yet classic design with just a hint of pop to celebrate her ever-growing family, Sherry chose a black-and-white, retro-style patterned paper which she accentuated with a red pen. Round and robust curves capture the shape of both the title number and baby belly, creating a visual flow and evoking a sense of joyful anticipation.

FAMILY OF 6 *by Sherry Wright*

Supplies: Patterned paper, rub-on definition, scalloped note card (Jenni Bowlin); chipboard letter, stamp (Heidi Swapp); chipboard number (BasicGrey); Misc: ink, pen, transparency

Four Kids.
Who me?
Had you told me 6 years ago
I'd be the mother of 4
would have cried.

THE
AKERS
KIDS
Affair 4

But life without Emma
Would not be my life.
She completes us.
This Four Kid Family Affair

A family layout is an essential page to create, especially when a new addition arrives. Here, Ruth features her four beautiful children in a collage-style portrait. Try this look at home, beginning with a focal point image of your family. Frame each of your children's faces in the portrait with a metal-rimmed label holder. For repetition and depth, incorporate a second, similarly sized image of each child, setting the photos on adhesive foam squares. Using black-and-white images creates a unified look.

THE AKERS FAMILY *by Ruth Akers*

Supplies: Cardstock; eyelets, metal letters and accents, patterned paper, rub-ons (We R Memory Keepers); buttons, ribbon (American Crafts); Misc: adhesive foam

GETTING STARTED
scrapbooking

Your Guide to Creating Beautiful Baby Layouts

You've got plenty of baby photos and memorabilia, right? Then you're ready to start scrapping! All you really need to start recording those precious moments are a few basic supplies. The first few pages in this section will explain the essentials. Then turn the pages for guidelines and simple techniques for putting it all together.

basic tools *and* supplies

ORGANIZATION

Organizing digital photos is simple if you do it as you go. You can use photo organization software or even Windows Explorer. Take a few minutes at the end of every week or every month to organize baby photos into folders by date or topic. That way, you'll be able to quickly locate specific photos when the urge strikes to create a page.

Basic file folders and accordion files are great for sorting and storing printed photos, memorabilia and supplies like patterned paper. As with digital folders, these folders can be organized by date or topic. The most important thing is keep up with the sorting!

PAPER

Paper is arguably the most essential and versatile scrapbooking supply. Use it for layout backgrounds, decorative accents, photo corners, page borders, embellishments and more. The number of colors and patterns available will allow you to create an almost endless variety of adorable layouts. But don't be overwhelmed! Choosing soft colors and baby-themed papers will never fail you. And using papers from the same collection makes coordinating patterns a snap.

Patterned paper and cardstock are the paper types used predominantly for scrapbooking. Cardstock provides a heavy-weight background for a page—great for durability and holding heavy embellishments like buttons and large brads. But if you're putting a page in a sheet protector and storing it in an album, patterned paper works just as well for preserving memories. Both types of paper are available in solid colors or patterns and many come double-sided for extra versatility.

CUTTING TOOLS

A pair of scissors is all that's really required to cut paper. But several tools on the market make paper cutting so much easier. Slide paper trimmers allow you to quickly cut a straight line on a sheet of paper or cardstock. And many models are able to hold 12" x 12" (30cm x 30cm) sizes. Using a craft knife with a metal-edged ruler also works for cutting straight lines. (Just be sure to put a cutting mat under your paper to protect your work surface.) Other cutting tools that are great to have on hand include micro-tip scissors and paper punches. Micro-tip scissors are perfect for cutting around small designs like flowers and hearts. Paper punches make cutting out a variety of shapes easy as pie.

ADHESIVES

The number and types of adhesives available can make the task of choosing one a bit daunting. Have no fear! Just follow these guidelines: For basic pages, glue sticks, double-sided tape and tape runners all work well for attaching paper or photos to paper. For more dimensional embellishments (like ribbon, buttons and tags) glue dots and glue lines provide a solid bond. Over time, you'll figure out which adhesives you prefer. But it's always handy to have both wet and dry adhesives in your collection.

EMBELLISHMENTS

You can easily create a page with just paper and
photos. But embellishments really make layouts
pop—literally. An embellishment is just like its
name suggests: a decorative item that embellishes
a page. Embellishments are typically three
dimensional, like buttons, brads, eyelets, ribbon
and chipboard. Embellishments add style,
personality and texture to a page, and can take
a simple layout to the next level. Found objects,
office supplies, or whatever you have lying around
the house can potentially decorate a page. And don't
forget the letters! Letter stickers (which come in a
variety of sizes, styles and materials), chipboard and
rub-ons make creating titles quick, easy and fun.

ALBUMS

Albums are sold in a variety of styles including post-bound,
spiral bound, strap-style and three-ring binder. Most
popular for scrapbook pages are the 8.5" x 11" (22cm
x 28cm) and 12" x 12" (30cm x 30cm) sizes. But
mini albums are also popular for holding small
scrapbook layouts. Albums should provide and
acid- and lignin-free environment for photos
and mementos.

*Note: For preservation purposes we recommend the use of
acid- and lignin-free paper products, as well as photo-safe
adhesives.*

designing a layout

Your baby photos are just screaming to get on a page. Now what? There are no hard and fast rules for creating a layout—whatever style you like (whether it's classic, modern or anything goes) can be re-created on a page. But regardless of style, it helps to follow some general guidelines when putting together your layouts.

INSPIRATION

Before you even start designing your layout, think about the look you want to create and how you might want to arrange your page. Ideas abound for layout designs. Scrapbook magazines and Web sites have tons of layout ideas and several include page maps (sketches) for helping you re-create specific layout designs. And don't forget—this book is chock full of fantastic ideas for re-creating layouts. Spend some time flipping through the pages and note which designs you might want to try out.

PICKING A FOCAL POINT

Choose a photo or two to be the focus of the layout, to capture the readers' attention and ground the layout's design. The focal point photo should be more prominent (either in placement or size) to any other photos in the layout.

Here, making the focal point photo larger than the other photos helps it stand out.

CREATING BALANCE

It's important for a layout to be visually balanced. But "balanced" doesn't necessarily mean symmetrical. Using colors of the same intensity (like bright pink and orange) creates balance. Adding embellishments of the same visual weight (such as eyelets and delicate ribbon) creates balance. And using a visual triangle—a design that leads the eye in a triangle around the page—also creates balance.

The three flower embellishments on this layout create a visual triangle.

CHOOSING COLOR

The most straightforward way to choose coordinating colors is to use a color wheel. You can also look around for inspiration—nature, your living room, a magazine ad. Be sure to choose colors that complement each other as well as the layout's focal point photo, whether they match the colors in a picture or create a mood for the page.

The colors in this layout are drawn from the photo, creating a cohesive and attractive design.

WRITING TEXT

The layout's title plays an important role; it should catch the viewer's interest and hint at the page's story. Journaling is another important element for a page. Whether it's a brief handwritten note or a typed paragraph, journaling adds detail and context to photos. If nothing else, jot down a short caption for a photo and the date. But it's even better to tell a story.

ADDING EMBELLISHMENTS

Think of embellishments as you would clothing accessories—they should complete the look, enhance the page and complement the design. If in doubt about how much to add, "less is more" is a good philosophy and keeps embellishments from taking away from the page's focal point.

Take a look at the following pages for basic techniques and easy ways to embellish your layouts.

Just a few embellishments—the flowers and brads—are all that's needed to enhance the feminine look of this page.

SIMPLE *scrapbooking* tECHNIQUES

Now that you're stocked with photos and supplies, follow these super simple techniques for creating precious and pretty pages.

APPLYING RUB-ONS

Rub-on transfers are a must-have for adding cute designs to your pages. They are available in a variety of designs, colors and fonts. Like stickers, rub-ons come in sheets, but once the image is rubbed onto the paper, it looks just like it's part of the surface.

Supplies: rub-ons, scissors, craft stick or bone folder

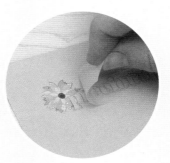

1 With scissors, cut out just the image you want to transfer.

2 Remove the paper backing, and place the image on the paper with the faded side down. Using a craft stick or bone folder, rub the plastic backing, making sure to rub over the entire image.

3 Slowly peel off the plastic backing to reveal the transfer. If any part of the image did not transfer, put the plastic back down and rub over it again.

A NOTE ABOUT INKING EDGES

Adding a bit of ink to the edges of photos, embellishments and background paper adds a finished look and a soft touch to a page, perfect for pages with sweet baby faces. To ink the edges of your papers, simply hold your inkpad in one hand and your paper in the other, then move the edge of the paper along the surface of the ink pad.

SETTING EYELETS

Delicate little eyelets are perfect additions to a precious baby page. They're great for attaching paper embellishments or just for adding dimension. Once you've got the right tools, setting eyelets is simple.

Supplies: eyelets, eyelet setter, hole punch, cutting mat, craft hammer

1 Punch a hole in your paper the same size as your eyelet. (The standard size is ¹⁄₁₆" [2mm].)

2 Insert the eyelet into the hole and turn the paper over so that the flat side of the eyelet is on your craft mat.

3 Insert the pointy tip of your setter into the long end of the eyelet. While holding the setter upright and steady, gently tap the end of the setter with your craft hammer a few times. If needed, you can then remove the setter and tap directly on the eyelet to flatten it.

ATTACHING BRADS

Brads come in an array of sizes, shapes and yummy colors, and they serve a similar purpose to that of eyelets. Use them to attach flowers and tags, as bullet points for journaling or as their own design. Plus, brads require only one simple tool, so attaching them is a snap.

Supplies: brad, ¹⁄₁₆" (2mm) hole punch or paper piercer

 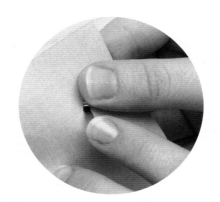

1 Poke a hole (with the hole punch or paper piercer) in your paper where you want to place the brad.

2 Insert the brad into the hole. Be sure to insert the brad into anything that is being attached (such as a flower) before inserting the brad in the hole on the page. Then bend the prongs to secure the brad in place.

GETTING THE PERFECT STAMPED IMAGE

Stamps are a quick way to add images to your layout. Use them to decorate the background paper or make your own embellishments. Materials are simple—just a stamp and ink! Getting a crisp, solid stamp image is easy using the following technique.

First, lay your stamp on its back, and lightly tap the ink pad on the stamp's image. This will help keep the ink on the image and off the stamp's background. Repeat the tapping until the image is completely inked. Then turn the stamp over and press it on your paper evenly. Don't rock the stamp back and forth. Lift the stamp straight up to remove. Let the ink dry before adding any color to the image.

ALL ABOUT CHIPBOARD

Chipboard is a type of cardboard used by scrapbookers to embellish a page. Some chipboard is decorated and self-adhesive, which is great for quickly making pages. Other chipboard comes undressed (plain), allowing you to customize it to match a layout. You can use whatever adhesive you like to attach chipboard. Try these simple steps for decorating your chipboard—dressed or ready-made.

MAKING CHIPBOARD SHINE

Supplies: undressed chipboard, acrylic paint, brush, dimensional adhesive or iridescent medium

1 Brush acrylic paint over the piece and allow it to try.

2 Brush a thin layer of shiny liquid such as dimensional adhesive (like Diamond Glaze) or iridescent medium (found at art supply stores) over dried paint.

ADDING PATTERN TO CHIPBOARD

Supplies: chipboard, decoupage medium, brush, craft knife

1 Brush decoupage medium on the front of your chipboard. Then attach the chipboard, facedown, to the back of a sheet of patterned paper. Allow the decoupage medium to dry.

2 With a craft knife, cut out the paper around the chipboard. You can sand or add ink to the edges of the chipboard to create a distressed look.

WORKING WITH RIBBON

Want to add color, texture and dimension to your layout? Try adding ribbon! Ribbon is so versatile that baby girl and boy pages alike will benefit. Glue dots are an excellent method of securing ribbon to paper, but double-sided tape and tape runners also do the trick. Trimming the ends of ribbon at an angle will keep the ribbon from fraying.

Stuck on what to do with your ribbon? Try these techniques.

Tie ribbon onto a tag or another embellishment. Just punch a hole to turn any paper embellishment into a tag.

Adhere ribbon to the edges of a photo to act as a frame. Or add triangles of ribbon for photo corners.

Attach strips of ribbon to embellish a page. Add brads or staples to the ribbon for a more masculine look; add flowers for a feminine feel.

SOURCE GUIDE

The following companies manufacture products featured in this book. Please check your local retailers to find these materials, or go to a company's Web site for the latest product. In addition, we have made every attempt to properly credit the items mentioned in this book. We apologize to any company that we have listed incorrectly, and we would appreciate hearing from you.

3L Corporation
(800) 828-3130
www.scrapbook-adhesives.com

7gypsies
(877) 749-7797
www.sevengypsies.com

A2Z Essentials
(419) 663-2869
www.geta2z.com

Adobe Systems Incorporated
(800) 833-6687
www.adobe.com

Adornit/Carolee's Creations
(435) 563-1100
www.adornit.com

All My Memories
(888) 553-1998
www.allmymemories.com

American Crafts
(801) 226-0747
www.americancrafts.com

Arctic Frog
(479) 636-3764
www.arcticfrog.com

Around The Block
(801) 593-1946
www.aroundtheblockproducts.com

Autumn Leaves
(800) 588-6707
www.autumnleaves.com

BAM POP LLC
www.bampop.com

BasicGrey
(801) 544-1116
www.basicgrey.com

Bazzill Basics Paper
(480) 558-8557
www.bazzillbasics.com

Berwick Offray, LLC
(800) 344-5533
www.offray.com

Bo-Bunny Press
(801) 771-4010
www.bobunny.com

Chatterbox, Inc.
(888) 416-6260
www.chatterboxinc.com

CherryArte
(212) 465-3495
www.cherryarte.com

Collage Press
(435) 676-2039
www.collagepress.com

Colorbök, Inc.
(800) 366-4660
www.colorbok.com

Cosmo Cricket
(800) 852-8810
www.cosmocricket.com

Costco Wholesale Corporation
www.costco.com

Craft ROBO/Graphtec Corporation
www.graphteccorp.com

Crafter's Workshop, The
(877) 272-3837
www.thecraftersworkshop.com

Crate Paper
(801) 798-8996
www.cratepaper.com

Creating Keepsakes
(888) 247-5282
www.creatingkeepsakes.com

Creative Imaginations
(800) 942-6487
www.cigift.com

Dafont
www.dafont.com

Daisy Bucket Designs
(541) 289-3299
www.daisybucketdesigns.com

Daisy D's Paper Company
(888) 601-8955
www.daisydspaper.com

Darice, Inc.
(800) 321-1494
www.darice.com

DECAdry PC Papers
www.decadry.com

Dèjá Views
(800) 243-8419
www.dejaviews.com

Deluxe Designs
(480) 497-9005
www.deluxecuts.com

Designer Digitals
www.designerdigitals.com

Designfruit
www.designfruit.com

Die Cuts With A View
(801) 224-6766
www.diecutswithaview.com

Digi Shoppe, The
www.thedigishoppe.com

Digital Design Essentials
www.digitaldesignessentials.com

Digital Scrapbook Memories
(801) 983-4946
www.digitalscrapbookmemories.com

Dollarama—*no source available*

Doodlebug Design Inc.
(877) 800-9190
www.doodlebug.ws

Dream Street Papers
(480) 275-9736
www.dreamstreetpapers.com

Dymo
(800) 426-7827
www.dymo.com

EK Success, Ltd.
(800) 524-1349
www.eksuccess.com

Eyelet Outlet
(618) 622-9741
www.eyeletoutlet.com

EZ Actions by Photoblast
(469) 667-5280
www.ezactions.com

Fancy Pants Designs, LLC
(801) 779-3212
www.fancypantsdesigns.com

Fontwerks
(604) 942-3105
www.fontwerks.com

Frances Meyer, Inc.
(413) 584-5446
www.francesmeyer.com

Funky Playground Designs
www.funkyplaygrounddesigns.com

Gina Miller Designs
www.ginamillerdesigns.com

Hambly Studios
(800) 451-3999
www.hamblystudios.com

Heidi Grace Designs, Inc.
(866) 348-5661
www.heidigrace.com

Heidi Swapp/Advantus Corporation
(904) 482-0092
www.heidiswapp.com

Hero Arts Rubber Stamps, Inc.
(800) 822-4376
www.heroarts.com

Hobby Lobby Stores, Inc.
www.hobbylobby.com

Imagination Project, Inc.
(888) 477-6532
www.imaginationproject.com

Imaginisce
(801) 908-8111
www.imaginisce.com

Jen Wilson Designs
www.jenwilsondesigns.com

Jenni Bowlin
www.jennibowlin.com

Jesse James & Co., Inc.
(610) 435-0201
www.jessejamesbutton.com

Jo-Ann Stores
www.joann.com

Junkitz
(732) 792-1108
www.junkitz.com

K&Company
(888) 244-2083
www.kandcompany.com

Karen Russell
www.karenrussell.typepad.com

KI Memories
(972) 243-5595
www.kimemories.com

Kodomo, Inc.
(650) 685-1828
www.kodomoinc.com

Krylon
(800) 457-9566
www.krylon.com

Lazar Studiowerx, Inc.
(866) 478-9379
www.lazarstudiowerx.com

Li'l Davis Designs
(480) 223-0080
www.lildavisdesigns.com

Lilypad, The
www.the-lilypad.com

Little Dreamer Designs
www.littledreamerdesigns.com

Making Memories
(801) 294-0430
www.makingmemories.com

Martha Stewart Crafts
www.marthastewartcrafts.com

May Arts
(800) 442-3950
www.mayarts.com

Maya Road, LLC
(214) 488-3279
www.mayaroad.com

Melissa Frances/Heart & Home, Inc.
(888) 616-6166
www.melissafrances.com

Michaels Arts & Crafts
(800) 642-4235
www.michaels.com

Microsoft Corporation
www.microsoft.com

My Mind's Eye, Inc.
(800) 665-5116
www.mymindseye.com

Natural Designs in Scrapbooking
www.ndisb.com

Nunn Design
(800) 761-3557
www.nunndesign.com

October Afternoon
www.octoberafternoon.com

Offray—*see Berwick Offray, LLC*

One Heart...One Mind, LLC
(888) 414-3690

Paper Salon
(800) 627-2648
www.papersalon.com

Paper Studio
(480) 557-5700
www.paperstudio.com

Pebbles Inc.
(801) 235-1520
www.pebblesinc.com

Pressed Petals
(800) 748-4656
www.pressedpetals.com

Prima Marketing, Inc.
(909) 627-5532
www.primamarketinginc.com

Provo Craft
(800) 937-7686
www.provocraft.com

Queen & Co.
(858) 613-7858
www.queenandcompany.com

QuicKutz, Inc.
(888) 702-1146
www.quickutz.com

Rhonna Designs
www.rhonnadesigns.com

Rusty Pickle
(801) 746-1045
www.rustypickle.com

Scenic Route Paper Co.
(801) 542-8071
www.scenicroutepaper.com

ScrapArtist
(734) 717-7775
www.scrapartist.com

Scrapbook Answers - *no longer in business*

Scrapbook-Bytes
(607) 642-5391
www.scrapbook-bytes.com

Scrapbook-Elements
www.scrapbook-elements.com/sbe

Scrapbook Graphics
www.scrapbookgraphics.com

Scrapsupply
(615) 777-3953
www.scrapsupply.com

Scrapworks, LLC / As You Wish Products, LLC
(801) 363-1010
www.scrapworks.com

Second Mile Freebies
www.second-mile-freebies.blogspot.com

SEI, Inc.
(800) 333-3279
www.shopsei.com

Shabby Princess
www.shabbyprincess.com

Sizzix
(877) 355-4766
www.sizzix.com

Stampin' Up!
(800) 782-6787
www.stampinup.com

Staples, Inc.
www.staples.com

Sugarloaf Products, Inc.
(770) 484-0722
www.sugarloafproducts.com

Sweet Shoppe Designs
www.sweetshoppedesigns.com

Sweetwater
(800) 359-3094
www.sweetwaterscrapbook.com

Technique Tuesday, LLC
(503) 644-4073
www.techniquetuesday.com

Three Bugs in a Rug, LLC
(801) 804-6657
www.threebugsinarug.com

Tin Box Creations
www.tinboxcreations.com

Tinkering Ink
(877) 727-2784
www.tinkeringink.com

Two Peas in a Bucket
(888) 896-7327
www.twopeasinabucket.com

We R Memory Keepers, Inc.
(801) 539-5000
www.weronthenet.com

Westrim Crafts
(800) 727-2727
www.westrimcrafts.com

WorldWin Papers
(888) 834-6455
www.worldwinpapers.com

Wrights Ribbon Accents
(877) 597-4448
www.wrights.com

Zsiage, LLC
(718) 224-1976
www.zsiage.com

INDEX

FOR MORE IDEAS AND TECHNIQUES, CHECK OUT THESE OTHER MEMORY MAKERS BOOKS.

See what's coming up from Memory Makers Books by checking out our blog: *www.memorymakersmagazine.com/booksblog/*

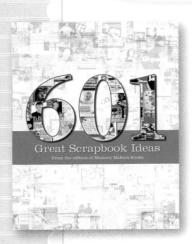

601 GREAT SCRAPBOOK IDEAS

Brimming with inspiration and ideas, you'll discover one amazing page after another in this big book of layouts.

ISBN-13: 978-1-59963-017-5
ISBN-10: 1-59963-017-6

Paperback
272 pages
Z1640

These books and other fine Memory Makers books are available at your local scrapbook retailer, bookstore or online supplier or visit our Web site at www.memorymakersmagazine.com or www.mycraftivity.com

FIND YOUR GROOVE

Kitty Foster and Wendy McKeehan take you on a journey to discovering your own scrapbook style through quizzes, exercises, challenges and page after page of fabulous layouts sure to inspire.

ISBN-13: 978-1-59963-006-9
ISBN-10: 1-59963-006-0

Paperback
112 pages
Z0787

SCRAP SIMPLE

Scrapbooking doesn't have to be fussy to be fun! *Scrap Simple* makes it easy to whip up clean and uncluttered scrapbook pages in a flash.

ISBN-13: 978-1-59963-014-4
ISBN-10: 1-59963-014-1

Paperback
128 pages
Z1282

TODDLERHOOD

Find 150 fresh scrapbook pages and projects that document the frenetic fun of growing and learning in the toddler years.

ISBN-13: 978-1-59963-007-6
ISBN-10: 1-59963-007-9

Paperback
128 pages
Z0788